At Night

AT
NIGHT

DUKE WILLS

AT NIGHT

DIXE WILLS

Published by AA Publishing, a trading name of
AA Media Limited, Fanum House, Basing View,
Basingstoke, Hampshire RG21 4EA, UK.

www.theAA.com

First published in 2015
10 9 8 7 6 5 4 3 2 1

A CIP catalogue record for this book is available
from the British Library.

ISBN: 978-0-7495-7709-4

Illustrations by Harriet Yeomans
Typeset in Bembo Regular 12pt

Printed in Great Britain by Clays Ltd, St Ives plc

A04849

'Night is a world lit by itself.'

Antonio Porchia

For K

Contents

Preamble 9

. . ✦ . .

PART ONE ✦ LANDSCAPE

1 **Moorland** 19
2 **Island** 51
3 **Forest** 83
4 **Mountain** 113
5 **Sky** 139

PART TWO ✦ TRAVEL

6 **Train** 163
7 **Bicycle** 197
8 **Boots** 229

. . ✦ . .

Ten Night Rambling Tips 265
Train Travel Info 267
Bibliography & Websites 270
Author's Acknowledgements 271

Preamble

Night is a magician. A place familiar to us in daylight can seem suddenly strange and unknown beneath the velvet cape of darkness – a whole new mysterious entity brought into being by some subterfuge of the dark arts. Taking a trip out into the night, particularly in remoter spots where its power is not diminished by artificial light, is perhaps the closest we'll ever come to entering a magic kingdom of trickery and illusion.

A night spent out and about also offers a refreshing break from everyday life. It can even change the way we operate as humans as the usual hierarchy of our senses is turned upside down. Our eyes fail us in the gloom, while our ears and nose come into their own, picking up sounds and smells that are often masked in the daytime. Our sense of touch is also heightened when stripped of the visual signals we habitually rely on. The bark of a tree caressed in the dark of the night is a landscape all of its own.

Every year, around full moon, I take a group of people for a nocturnal wander around a beguiling corner of Suffolk to teach them some night-walking skills. On an 8-mile ramble that starts just as the last of dusk's light is giving out, we set off along a stretch of river whose mudflats release a pungent, almost primordial scent flecked with hints of ozone from the nearby sea. Gulls, geese and waders call their goodnights and we set our course by the flashing of distant river-mouth lights, green and red, and by an illuminated church tower rising from an old-fashioned seaside resort.

Passing the skeleton of an abandoned water pump, dramatically lit by the moon's reflection on the water, we follow a creek before diving into a little natural maze. Our maps become redundant among the high hedges of gorse and we must keep an eye on the stars to ensure we do not go around in circles. Coming at last to an elegant Victorian pier we wander along the shore, passing the ghostly forms of night anglers on the shingle beach. We forge a way back inland, pick our way over a thrillingly chilling cold sink of marshland, using the lights of a pub on the river to guide us. Crossing the waterway by an old bailey bridge, we head across heathland where our hearts leap into our mouths every time a panicked pheasant springs out at us. In dense woods, we hear the calls of hunting owls, before tramping out on a boardwalk over a sea of reeds, chalk white in the moonlight. We end our walk in a tiny village whose church bears the claw marks of the terrible hound of the marshes, Black Shuck. With any luck, we will not have encountered him on our way round.

En route I attempt to teach the group some tricks to help them find their way by night, when many landmarks will have disappeared from view. We all have a go at navigating by the stars, and use our ears and noses to help us stay on the right path. As we amble along, I also try to weave in my top ten – one must *always* have ten – night rambling tips (reproduced on page 265). I'm not sure how much of any of this goes in because from a very early stage most of the party are wrapped in a sort of entranced awe at the night and its beauties, as seen both on the ground and in the sky above us. I don't have to teach people to appreciate the night because for almost everyone it is something that comes completely naturally and they find themselves both surprised and delighted at how they feel.

It is strange then that we humans tend to associate the night with evil and have done so for far longer than we have nursed within our breast any conception of right and wrong. Our prehistoric forebears will have recognised all too well that, though the nocturnal hours brought with them a shroud that conveniently concealed their own wrongdoings, the darkness also provided the opportunity for others, whether human or animal, to harm them. The comfort that could be gained from a fire at night came not only from its warmth but also the light it cast into the bewildering and frightening darkness where death could take a person unawares in an instant.

Even in modern-day Britain this belief that evil lurks in the darkness shows no signs of dying out.

At Night

It is a notion espoused in many areas of our culture, from virtually every horror film ever made, to the ghost trains at the fairground, to the movement-sensitive lights attached to our houses, to the service of compline, the final prayers of the day, when monks, nuns and sundry faithful appeal to God to defend them from 'evil dreams' and the 'fears and terrors of the night'.

I confess that I myself often feel a vague apprehension before spending the night roaming about alone. It comes upon me at twilight, the time the French call *entre chien et loup* – 'between dog and wolf'. It's a phrase that imagines the changing of the guard between the kingdom of the animals of the light and the – by inference – much more dangerous and anarchic world of their nocturnal cousins. If I've learnt anything from the nights I've spent at large, the danger and the anarchy tend not to be found in the darkness itself but in our wild imaginings of what might happen to us simply because we cannot see. We are not apt to find our way around by smell, as the badger does, nor are we highly sensitised to vibrations like the mole. We do not possess the acute hearing of the bat, nor (and this is probably a blessing) do we use our tongues for navigation as is the wont of many snakes. So when we are deprived of our sight we often go a little to pieces, particularly if we are urban souls and accustomed to street lamps stepping into the breach when the sun goes down.

The unsettling sense of trepidation soon leaves me though. I liken it to the experience of meeting someone new – most of us don't feel quite relaxed in another's company until we've got to know them a little. Similarly, once I've spent half an hour or so in the night's presence and have scraped acquaintance, the patina of disquiet melts away. I've found it's not enough to have befriended The Night in general because each night is a new character who demands that I get to know it on its own terms. That's not to say that, even when I feel at home with it, it won't have a few tricks up its sleeve – as any self-respecting magician would.

I have written this book partly to dispel some of the fear that many of us feel about the night. I also wanted to share some of the very different night-time experiences that Britain has to offer, in the hope that readers will come to know some of their joys themselves.

Colliding head on with the notion of the night as a place of evil, I begin on Dartmoor where the Devil himself is said to ride out with his terrible red-eyed hounds, bringing untimely death to all who encounter him. On Skomer, I become immersed in what is at once one of Britain's most spectacular avian events and a titanic battle for survival. The island is home to up to a million Manx shearwaters, a plucky little seabird who, night after night every summer, runs a deadly gauntlet in a selfless bid to feed its young. The ensuing bedlam is like nothing else I've ever known.

At Sherwood, I attempt to find shelter for the night in one of England's great ancient forests beneath oaks that have seen darkness fall 250,000 times or more. I enjoy chance meetings with other wild creatures of the wood and, when calamity strikes, a modern-day Robin Hood sweeps to my rescue. Heading west to Cadair Idris in Snowdonia I experience the transformative power of the night and test out the myth that anyone who spends the hours of darkness alone on the summit comes down magically metamorphosed into either a poet or a lunatic.

Pressing northward to Scotland, I come to the Galloway Forest Park, the UK's first Dark Sky Park, where light pollution has been banned and the heavens can be seen as our ancestors saw them, in all their sparkling glory.

The second part of this book is devoted to three different forms of nocturnal travel. First, I spend the night awake on the sleeper train from Fort William in the Highlands down to London. I cycle back out of London to the Suffolk Coast on the Dunwich Dynamo, a 115-mile overnight ride for which neither the route nor, as I discover, my bicycle is prepared. Finally, I follow in the footsteps of an insomniac Charles Dickens to investigate the life that goes on in the capital while its population sleeps.

Naturally, there's no obligation for readers to follow in my own footsteps or to seek out any other nocturnal adventures of their own. They may instead prefer to live out such experiences vicariously through these pages. However, I would encourage everyone who comes across this book to gird their loins and step outside into the darkness of the night (which, to be honest, is very rarely truly dark in Britain), for if we do not encounter the night, we reduce the realm we inhabit by roughly a third. Furthermore, we will never know if the world at three in the morning is actually an improvement on the world at three in the afternoon. We will rarely get to meet the wildlife that sleeps under the sun and roams by moonlight. We will not become acquainted with that particular stillness that sometimes comes at night, nor allow the senses other than our sight free rein to show us what they can do.

Perhaps most importantly of all, if we do venture out, we will discover that the night is not a place to be feared but to be embraced, a place where everything is fundamentally the same but nothing is actually quite the same. To misquote L P Hartley for a moment, 'The night is a magical country: they do things differently there.'

PART ONE
LANDSCAPE

1

Moorland

The Devil rides out on Dartmoor. Or at least he does at night – as one might expect of someone who styles himself the Prince of Darkness. This means that if you wish to see the Devil face to face – which, as we shall see, is seldom desirable – you'll have to venture out on the moor after dusk.

You can't just ramble about any old patch of moor either. Of the 368 square miles available to him, the Devil – or the Dewer, as he is often known locally – has shown himself partial to a particular slice of Dartmoor that stretches from the southeast corner by Shaugh Prior to a spot roughly at the centre, just beyond Two Bridges. Accounts of his sorties in these parts suggest that his home within this hunting ground is a small patch of trees known as Wistman's Wood. Since the night has traditionally been held to be the time when wickedness runs amok, I felt it behoved me to confront it at the place the very Crown Prince of Evil has apparently chosen for an earthly abode. For good or ill, Wistman's Wood was where

At Night

I would keep vigil until the morning to beard him in his den. Should the Devil not show his face, I would have to hope that I would come away with some inkling that might help unravel the mystery of how generation after generation of moorland folk became obsessed with the idea that, when the sun went down, he lived among them, leading a pack of hounds that were, if anything, even more terrifying a prospect than the Devil himself.

Was it that Wistman's Wood caused the wind to make a diabolical screech as it blew through its branches? Was there some sort of rare lichen on the trees that glowed beneath the starlight to mimic the eyes of slavering dogs? Or perhaps there was simply something deeply sinister about the wood that could not be explained away? There are, after all, plenty of places around the country that have gained a reputation as the hosts of mystifying phenomena, often ascribed to the activities of restless spirits, poltergeists or some sort of demonic force.

I'm not an unusually timid person. I have, on several occasions, happened to find myself sleeping alone in supposedly haunted rooms – once in a four-poster bed said to be assailed nightly by a whole pantheon of ghosts. However, as I made my way towards Dartmoor I have to confess that I harboured the hope that, if I were to come across anything out of the ordinary that night, it might be something whose source was more obviously natural than supernatural.

I began my journey on a pleasant July afternoon, grinding my way slowly up onto the moor on my bicycle from the market town of Tavistock. As my back grumbled and muttered and, at length, began to whine rather pathetically, I contented myself that this potentially spirit-crushing climb had been arranged for the good of my soul, a part of me that benefits from a gentle harrowing from time to time. At 2,039ft, Dartmoor's highest point – the appropriately named High Willhays – is less than 50ft shy of Kinder Scout, which is as high as you can go in the whole of the Peak District. If you've hauled yourself up onto the moor from one of the many towns that shelter below it, all illusions you may have cherished about Dartmoor's size and height are swiftly washed away in a tidal wave of sweat.

The climb also afforded me time to reflect on my own feelings about the Devil. I do not kid myself that I am any less capable of doing bad things – what the Church would call being sinful – than anyone else is. Say what you like about the Devil, but if he exists he at least serves as a mightily convenient bogey man whom I might blame for leading me into temptation. If he does not exist, and there is no great force tempting me to do wrong, then I alone am responsible for whatever I think, say and do. (I'm blithely and possibly rashly assuming here that I do not choose to blame my wrongdoings on society or my upbringing or whatever else instead.)

At Night

In any case, the Devil who rides out on Dartmoor is not a tempter. He does not offer a Faustian pact to those he comes across. He is a mere bringer of death. Thus I did not have to wonder whether I would be able to resist whatever temptation he might lay before me – there would be no offer, for example, to turn stones into bread (I had plenty of food with me anyway). There would simply be a harvesting of my soul for eternal damnation, which, as ends to camping trips go, would not count as a great result.

However, although it's all too easy to see that humans do evil things, I find it rather difficult to believe that there exists some sort of spirit who is the manifestation and source of all evil. That's not what I had been brought up to believe, mind you, and well into my adult life I'd have probably said there was such a creature, such is the power of beliefs inculcated at an early age. Even if I had still believed in such a being, though, I doubt I would have imagined myself running in terror from him and his dogs as they careered towards me over the moor.

Indeed, there was a greater danger. As the only being at Wistman's Wood tonight to recognise such concepts as good and evil and thus the only one capable of being the latter, the closest I might get to seeing the Devil was if I happened to catch sight of myself reflected in the river. This was not an encouraging thought.

Since I had no desire to get lost in the dark on my way to Wistman's Wood and thus risk the possibility of missing it altogether, I set out across the moor while there was still roughly an hour of light remaining in the day. I had left my bicycle in a tiny car park on the road between the hamlets of Two Bridges and Postbridge. The names testify to the importance of water crossings in this landscape scored with countless runnels, rills, leats and streams, and which is mother to the Dart, Erme, Plym, Meavy, Walkham, Tavy, Lyd, Okement, Taw, Teign, Bovey, Yealm and 13 other rivers besides. Having hopped, jumped, slithered, slipped and – as the last resort of a broken man – waded across many a moorland in the aftermath of a period of rain, I was thankful to be heading out onto Dartmoor in the middle of an unseasonably dry summer.

The bridleway that would take me to Wistman's Wood was the Lych Way, a route marked across my map with confident red dashes. It was a survivor from medieval times when the moorland folk would carry their dead along the path from their isolated and scattered homes for burial in the churchyard at Lydford, in those days a town of some importance spread about the walls of a fine castle. In summer such a journey – described with feeling by one venerable writer as 'eight miles in fair weather, and fifteen in foul' – would have been arduous enough. In winter, when the half dozen or more bridgeless streams and rivers along the path were in full spate, the venture took on nightmarish proportions, particularly if the long march had to be undertaken at night. In his seminal book on Devon, local historian Douglas St Leger-Gordon described how such nocturnal processions, illuminated by the flickering light of storm-lanterns, would have provided a more macabre and chilling sight to onlookers than any spectacle mere ghosts could have delivered.

Such excursions to far-off Lydford continued until the 13th century when Bishop Branscombe of Exeter annulled the regulation that the dead must be interred in their own parish churchyard and allowed them to be buried instead in the forest by Widecombe. This, of course, still entailed a trek across the moor, albeit one that no longer had to negotiate the Tavy, often claimed to be the fastest flowing river in England. It wasn't until 1868 that two so-called Chapels of Ease were built at Postbridge and Huccaby and the anxiety as to what might ensue in the wake of the death of a relative or neighbour could be excised from the list of fears faced by the isolated dwellers of the moor.

I knew, having tramped the 40-mile Lyke Wake Walk across the North York Moors by day and by night, that the reputation such 'corpse roads' have for disappearing into the mire just where it would be most useful to see a clear path is well deserved. It came as no surprise, therefore, when the Lych Way led me across a field and, cackling, dribbled away into it, leaving me to the tender mercies of a herd of cows not so much ready as eager to defend their calves to the death.

Passing warily onwards I came to a number of tall chimneys and roofless stone buildings that had the look of tiny Mayan temples. These were the relicts of mills that supplied gunpowder to Dartmoor's many mines and quarries in the latter half of the 19th century. I couldn't help thinking that producing explosives would be the sort of activity that would meet with the Devil's wholehearted approval. Not only were the works here the epitome of Blake's 'dark Satanic mills' but the mixture of saltpetre, charcoal and brimstone of which the 'black powder' was made reads like a list of the base elements of evil. Furthermore, where there was gunpowder there was always the gladdening prospect of premature death and the reaping of souls whose unrighteous owners had unwisely put off making them fit for the Other Place.

With good jobs at a premium on the moor in Victorian times, people came from far and wide to work here as carpenters, coopers, wheelwrights, blacksmiths and waggoners or, if they had none of these skills, as gunpowder makers. This last group, though in daily peril of their lives, at least had the consolation of knowing that if an explosion did transport them directly into hell, they'd barely notice a difference in their surroundings. It was only the invention of dynamite that brought this game of Russian roulette to an end, casting the entire workforce back out onto the moor to fend for themselves. Many would seek work and perhaps find death in the very mines and quarries they had helped to create.

I left the chimneys and mills behind, glad that I did not lift my head from the pillow each morning wondering whether I would be spared to rest my head on it at the end of the day. I made my way up and over Longaford Tor, a brief climb that found its reward in my first view of Wistman's Wood.

My initial feeling was that it was an underwhelming sort of place for the Devil to choose to live. Was this really the wood from which reckless midnight wanderers had witnessed his dramatic entrances onto the moor? Tucked meekly into the fold of a shallow valley of the West Dart River and stretching itself alongside the nascent waterway, it comprises two main copses, each a couple of hundred yards long, with a further little spinney cast adrift towards the north. The tallest among the trees measure no more than 30ft and the vast majority look up to them as giants. I had to keep reminding myself that since there are only three high-altitude oakwoods on the entire moor and Wistman's Wood is one of the highest in Britain, its mere existence is something of a marvel.

It was only when I closed in on the wood that I realised the great potential it had as a birthplace of legends. It was not windy enough to tell whether it could emit a diabolic shriek but it did seem just the sort of place the Devil would choose for a lair. The wood's stunted and deformed trees gave the impression that, at some time in the distant past, it had fallen victim to a terrible curse. Perhaps the inhabitants of a village that once existed here had displeased the Dewer in some way and so found themselves doomed to suffer forever, mutated into these grotesque imitations of trees? Their branches were so rich with lichen that it bulged off them like biceps. Flexing these parasite muscles, they struggled and strained to reach the sky but were forced out sideways in corkscrew contortions too painful to contemplate. I found photographs of the wood in winter in which they appeared like the tormented ghosts of trees. This being summer, the crowns were dressed in a shawl of green leaves, which did not mask their peculiarities but at least rendered them less dreadful to the eye.

This all made it rather less surprising that these apparently insignificant thickets are renowned as the most haunted place on Dartmoor. That's no mean achievement on a moor so thick with ghosts they are obliged to work to a strict rota to avoid the embarrassment of drifting through one another – the height of ill manners in the spectral world.

Had I passed this way 400 years ago I would have been met with an even more fantastical sight, for the trees then were described as being no taller than the height of a man. The climate in this valley has been less harsh over the last couple of centuries, allowing these same oaks – already of a good age when Charles II was restored to the throne – to grow to their current still rather less than dizzying heights. It means, of course, that when the medieval inhabitants of Dartmoor told the stories of the Devil riding out of Wistman's Wood, they may well have added the detail that he stood head and shoulders above the tops of the tallest trees.

Not unreasonably, given its rarity, the wood has been declared a Site of Special Scientific Interest and as such it is forbidden to enter it unless on official dendrological business. However, I reasoned that, should the Devil sweep out of the trees on a headless black charger in the midst of a pack of baying red-eyed Wisht Hounds, I would be unlikely to miss them should I spend the night just outside rather than just inside the wood. I set my tent up on the banks of the narrow river as the fading light began to play tricks with the gnarled, grasping fingers of the trees. I pricked up my ears to catch the first snarls and yelps of the Wisht Hounds.

Despite the fact that hounds are not nocturnal by nature, on Dartmoor these creatures share the Devil's predilection for roaming about during the hours of darkness. The name Wisht – sometimes written simply as Wish – is an old Devon word that has two discrete meanings, both of which might apply in the case of the hounds. The first denotes something along the lines of 'eerie' or 'uncanny'. Jet black dogs that are portrayed in story after story as spectral beings with murderous red eyes and a spine-chilling howl certainly live up to that billing. The second sense is that of being 'pixie-led'. This description opens a door upon a whole other world. Aside from the Dewer, the Wisht Hounds and ghosts in general, Dartmoor's other obsession is with pixies, or 'piskies' as they are known in the Devon dialect. As elsewhere in the world, the little people on Dartmoor are more inclined to mischief than pure evil, though they have been known to steal the odd baby. It appears the commonest way that people on the moor experienced a pixie was when they were unfortunate enough to be pixie-led.

Writing in 1890 in his all-encompassing work on the moor, William Crossing remarked that the superstition that anyone walking on Dartmoor could be led a merry dance by pixies 'seems to be the one which has longest continued to keep a hold upon the country people. There are many now in our villages, who while they would not admit that they believed in piskies' doings, yet are full of instances of folks having missed their way in the most mysterious manner, and are more ready to incline to the idea that supernatural agencies were at work, than to seek the actual causes of the mishaps.'

Typically the victim would be out walking across the moor when all at once they would lose track of time and become disorientated, no matter how well they might know the path. A mist might suddenly engulf them and an intense dizziness come upon them. Once released from the grip of the pixies' power, the episode would pass and they would come to their senses again. If the Wisht Hounds are indeed merely pixie-led, they cannot be held accountable for their actions, and are as innocent as the sleepwalker or the hypnotist's volunteer. However, that would mean that the pixies must be in league with the Devil, and though they might at times be rather trying, and the baby-stealing does cast something of a shadow over their moral standing, no one ever seems to have considered them to be demons. The Wisht Hounds, we must conclude, are simply bad – man's best friend become his worst nightmare.

The one thing the hounds cannot claim for themselves is that they are unique. Indeed, it would not be understating the case to say that Devon, and Dartmoor in particular, suffers from a plague of phantom black dogs who come out after dark. Several other packs of salivating, howling, scarlet-eyed hounds are said to step out at night, albeit at the command of lesser huntsmen than the Devil. Sir Francis Drake – a man at the centre of a bizarre set of legends including one in which he turns himself into a seagull to attack demons who are stealing his building materials – is said to go hunting with a spectral pack on Abbot's Way near his former home of Buckland Abbey. Death comes to any dog unfortunate enough to hear the cry of Drake's hounds. Over at Buckfastleigh, on the eastern side of the moor, another hunter and pack patrols a different section of the Abbot's Way. Further afield, a gentleman called Squire Arscott leads his curs through Tetcott Park. Then there is Squire Cabell, wicked *wicked* Squire Cabell, but we shall come to him later.

Despite their prevalence, the hounds who hunt in packs are almost certainly outnumbered by the solitary black dogs who make it their business to stand guard over bridges, gates, lanes and sundry other points of mild interest scattered throughout the county, with some of these creatures stoically overcoming the disability of their headlessness. They are typically of exceptional size and, if blessed with a head, stare out at the world through huge flaming eyes. With one exception – a pure white beast who was believed to haunt Cator Common near Widecombe – these hounds have coats of the purest sable, allowing them to merge with their night-darkened habitats in a satisfyingly sinister fashion.

One of the most notable among these solo black dogs appears in the fable of Lady Mary Howard. Legend has it that in life Lady Howard poisoned two of her four husbands and killed two of her children. As recompense for these crimes, her sin-charred ghost departs every night from the gateway of Fitzford House in Tavistock in a coach made of bones driven by an inevitably headless coachman. A huge black bloodhound runs in front of the carriage. In some versions of the tale, the carriage is empty and the cur is Lady Howard herself. Whichever is the case, the party always makes its gloomy way to the ruins of Okehampton Castle where Lady Howard plucks a single blade of grass from the lawn and returns to Fitzford House. This may seem an odd way to conduct one's affairs, even after death, but apparently she has been told that the only way she will be released from her earthly torment is if she can remove all the grass from Okehampton Castle at the rate of one blade per night.

This story held so much sway over the inhabitants of that district that parties broke up before midnight lest the revellers stray across Lady Howard as she went about her Sisyphean mission. It's a pity, really, that their festivities were halted on account of a tale based on such shaky ground. While it's a matter of record that Lady Mary did marry four times, she was apparently rather a pleasant person and, as pleasant persons are wont to do, abstained from killing any of her husbands or children no matter how irritating they were. Her history seems to have been mingled up somehow with that of another local Lady Howard whose first name was Frances and who was, by all accounts, not a person you would wish to meet in this world or indeed the next. It's striking, however, that even though neither woman is known to have owned any black dogs or be connected with them in any way in life, one still manages to take centre stage as soon as the legend dictates that there is to be a crossing of the moor at night.

Where this fixation with outsized black dogs came from is open to speculation. One possibility is that they owe their origin to Cerberus, the fearsome hound who kept watch over the gates of Hades. If so, that would certainly explain why Devon's supernatural dogs are always reported to be so large. However, as anyone with even a passing interest in Greek mythology will tell you, Cerberus was flush when it came to heads, having no fewer than three, which is two and sometimes three more than the county's own hounds.

It's also conceivable, of course, that there is no historical antecedent for the hounds. They may instead be nothing more than manifestations of the darker emotions that lurk in the shadowy corners of the human psyche. After all, it was not for nothing that Winston Churchill referred to the depressive turns that enveloped him as 'the black dog'.

More prosaically, they may simply be the fevered creation of generations of eyes peering anxiously into the mist or the darkness on the moor and seeing mighty hounds where, in the clear light of day, only rocky tors exist. Indeed, Hound Tor, which can be found some miles to the north of Wistman's Wood, is so called because it resembles a pack of hounds in full flight, apparently turned to stone by witches. It takes a little imagination to achieve this reverse metamorphosis from rock to canine flesh and blood but, given a foggy day or a timely cloud passing before the moon, they may well take on such forms, especially when the viewer has been primed to expect them.

What we can be sure of is that a very firmly held belief in the physical existence of the Wisht Hounds was widespread as recently as the 1870s, as is demonstrated by an intriguing case that came before a local coroner's jury. The men involved – such juries were all male in those days – were asked to pronounce on the cause of death of a man whose body was washed up on the banks of the River Yealm. Unable to determine what might have been the man's undoing, they came to the conclusion that he had been 'struck down by the phantom hunt'. It was quite natural then, given this reasoning, that they should return a verdict of 'death by supernatural agency'. It apparently took some considerable pressure from the powers that be before they grudgingly amended this verdict to one of 'accidental death'.

There were still curious incidents of the dogs in the night-time taking place several decades later. According to Ruth St Leger-Gordon, who with her aforementioned husband Douglas formed a formidable local history team, one such was revealed by a man who wrote to a local newspaper in 1958 about an unpleasant business that occurred during his childhood. He claimed that, after moving with his family to an old house between Widecombe and Postbridge – which puts it only a handful of miles to the east of Wistman's Wood – he was intimidated by a pack of black dogs who roamed around the courtyard and appeared intent on biting him. What made this event peculiar was that, though his mother and sister were also in the courtyard, neither of them could see the hounds. Presumably they were real enough to the boy though or he would hardly have gone to the trouble of writing to a newspaper about it many years later and opening himself up to the mocking scorn of its readership.

Was that a chill I felt down my spine as I screwed my eyes up in the gathering gloom thinking of that small boy surrounded by a pack of hounds no one but him could see? I stared at the anguished trees of Wistman's Wood until I could barely detect where the copse ended and the surrounding darkness began. The untidy scattered clouds of the day had drawn themselves together to fill the night sky so effectively that neither the gleam of the moon nor the sparkle from a single star penetrated the grey mantle they had formed. Yet somehow a light came from somewhere, for it was not pitch dark. I was in a slender valley with low hills to each side and hemmed in at the head and foot by more hills which had long since disappeared for the night. There was certainly no chance of any light coming from within this valley because the lonely little settlement that once stood here had withered away to nothing (for some other reason, I suspect, than having had its inhabitants turned into trees) and no one had found a convincing enough reason to live here since. I concluded that the faint light – little more than a rumour of light really – must be coming from over the hill in Princetown. The unblinking glare from the prison floodlights had perhaps deflected in off the clouds only to find its artificial radiance unwelcome here and so had limped off to peter out ineffectually among the rocks and stones and trees.

Standing alone underneath the sky, I was surprised to find myself mildly disappointed that there was not more of a frisson of something unholy in the air as the hours crept by. Indeed, the only element of the experience that felt at all uncanny was the unnatural stillness of the air. I don't know what I had expected in all honesty – a hint of sulphur on the breeze perhaps? I should have remembered that all horror movies begin with the unsuspecting victim imagining that everything is normal and nothing is amiss.

For want of anything better to do I strolled slowly about my impromptu campsite, a small triangle of grass bordered by the West Dart River – still nothing more than a rill here – and the Devonport leat, a shallow aqueduct dug in the late 18th century to carry drinking water down to the Devonport dockyards.

Suddenly I stopped stock still. Someone was out there in the darkness on the slopes of Longaford Tor. They had a radio on. This seemed remarkable because I hadn't seen a soul since I'd left the road several hours beforehand and I could not imagine why anyone would choose to tramp across the moor at night without apparently even bringing a torch to guide their way. I inclined my ear to the hubbub, which appeared to be coming from somewhere along the same Lych Way that had borne me here. When I listened more closely I could tell that the sound was not of music or chatter but that strain of white noise you get between radio stations.

I edged forward a little, heedful of the water running somewhere in front of me, and the noise stopped abruptly. All I could hear was the trickling and truckling of the stream before me and the less expansive rippling of the leat behind. Deciding that I must have imagined the radiophonic babel on the moor, I stepped forward again, only to find it starting up immediately. It didn't seem to be getting any nearer or going any further away. Someone was lurking out there, turning a de-tuned radio on and off. Even if the Devil and his Wisht Hounds didn't show their faces tonight, at least I could not complain of a lack of mysterious company.

I determined to investigate further and headed off towards the point where I could cross the stream. The scratchy noise duly disappeared. This gave me an idea, perhaps one that was rather overdue. I returned to the spot where I had first heard the radio. It magically came on again. I left. It went off. I smiled at my stupidity: the stream and the leat had played a little aural trick on me. Somehow they had arranged it so that their combined plashing and purling produced a noise that sounded like neither of them. My brain, knowing that it was unlikely that there was a radio close at hand, had reasoned that the noise must therefore be coming from somewhere out in the darkness, and the stationary stranger fiddling with an untuned radio was born. Suddenly I had a lot more sympathy for the people in the stories I had read who swore blind that they had heard the howling of vicious hounds on the moor and not just the moaning of the wind.

Returned to the normal world where no one takes it upon themselves to skulk about on a moor in the dark fiddling with a radio, I found everything deeply commonplace and shorn of the least hint of romance. The leat now whined in the manner of an extractor fan while the stream babbled on interminably like a broken cistern. To be honest, I preferred my fantasy world.

One winter, a friend and I spent a night camping on a mountainside in the Brecon Beacons in a snowstorm that lasted 12 hours. We lay awake in our tents punching the sides from time to time to keep the snow from collapsing our fragile coffin-sized homes. All night the wind raced up the valley and, as it turned the corner to pass us in our little cleft, it unleashed on the world a great reverberating boooooommm as if it were crashing its fist down on a mighty oak table in fury at some unknowable injustice perpetrated upon it.

Come the morning, we gingerly poked our heads out of our tents to discover that the snowstorm had exhausted itself at last. The wind had gone off to rage against the machine on some other mountainside and the sun was lighting up the walls of the ruined priory in the valley below us. The tranquillity of the scene made the storm of the night before seem dreamlike. Had it not been for the extra foot of snow that hadn't been there when we'd retreated into our burrows, the idea that we could have heard the wind indulging in such a terrible tantrum would have seemed ridiculous. However, at the time, had you told me that the noise was not that of the wind but of some demonic force come to wreak havoc on the world, I would have hesitated before denying it.

Nature finds it easier to play such tricks on us at night, of course, when we can no longer rely on our eyes to protect us from our innate gullibility. Had I heard the 'radio' in daylight, I like to think I would not have entertained the bizarre notion I formed for more than a second or two. Likewise, as I passed Longaford Tor in the last of the evening sunshine, at no point did it occur to me to consider that what I was looking at might not be an outcrop of rocks but rather a huddled pack of diabolical black hounds.

I've no doubt that it was night's way of conjuring the horrifying from the unremarkable that appealed to Sir Arthur Conan Doyle when in 1901 he visited friends near Buckfastleigh, a village on Dartmoor. However, the author of a dozen books on the subject of the afterlife did not take his inspiration for *The Hound of the Baskervilles* from the Wisht Hounds, as might be supposed, but from a set of dogs that accompany an even stranger fellow than the Devil. The dedication in his most famous work reads,

MY DEAR ROBINSON,

It was to your account of a West-Country legend that this tale owes its inception. For this, and for your help in the details all thanks.

Yours most truly,

A. CONAN DOYLE

HINDHEAD,
HASLEMERE

It's generally accepted that the story to which he refers was that of Squire Cabell.

Cabell is noted for being a particularly wicked squire, even by 17th-century standards. Several accounts have him selling his soul to the Devil, though one can't help thinking that this is a version of events given by his contemporaries in an attempt to explain his extreme villainy and perhaps distance themselves from any notion that they could be capable of sinking so low themselves. We actually know very little about his life aside from his apparent black-heartedness; that he was an avid huntsman; and that, just before he died, he was attended by a pack of ghostly hounds who had come to escort his soul to hell.

An indication of how Cabell was perceived by the local community can be gleaned from what happened immediately after his death in 1677. His body was taken to the graveyard at Holy Trinity Church in Buckfastleigh where his coffin was set in the ground and a large stone laid on top of it. This was not a tombstone placed with reverence for the newly departed but rather served as a way of keeping the coffin lid down to prevent Cabell, about whose death there was not a shadow of doubt, from pushing it open and climbing back out. In case this measure was not safeguard enough, to make absolutely certain that the malevolent squire never troubled anyone again, a block of stone the size and shape of an altar was positioned on top. Clearly perturbed that this might still not be sufficient, the people of Buckfastleigh then built a porch to cover the grave and closed it up with thick iron bars and a stout oak door. The resulting monument – surely one of the most damning memorials to anyone's life ever created – is still there in the churchyard for all to wonder at. This is more than can be said for most of the church, which was deliberately burnt down one night in 1992 by a fire started beneath the altar. The arsonists were rumoured to be Devil worshippers, though their identities have never been discovered.

Of course, all the precautions taken by the God-fearing folk of Buckfastleigh back in 1677 proved to no avail. Whenever the village is visited by a night when thunder and lightning rend the heavens, the spectral hounds return to the tomb to bay and howl until the ghostly form of Squire Cabell rises once more to join them for a hunt across the moor.

One imagines that Conan Doyle, who devoted a great deal of his time to the study of life after death and spent a colossal £250,000 promoting spiritualism, would have given anything to have caught a glimpse of the spirit of Richard Cabell charging across the moor with his faithful hounds in search of appetising quarry. However, he had to make do with Robinson's account of the legend followed by an extensive tour of the moor, taking in its isolated homesteads and perilous mires. The guide who accompanied him on this journey was a young coachman named Harry Baskerville.

Fired up by the striking scenery, the bone-chilling Squire Cabell tale and the dramatic possibilities of setting large parts of his story in the dead of the night, Conan Doyle sent his acerbic sleuth onto the moor to unravel what would become his most famous case. However, it's clear from the following conversation between Holmes and Watson that Conan Doyle had also been briefed about the Devil's own hunting activities in the locality. The detective opens the exchange:

> '...Here are two moorland farmhouses, High Tor and
> Foulmire. Then fourteen miles away the great convict
> prison of Princetown. Between and around these
> scattered points extends the desolate, lifeless moor.
> This, then, is the stage upon which tragedy has
> been played, and upon which we may help to play
> it again.'
> 'It must be a wild place.'
> 'Yes, the setting is a worthy one. If the devil did desire
> to have a hand in the affairs of men—'
> 'Then you are yourself inclining to the supernatural
> explanation.'
> 'The devil's agents may be of flesh and blood, may
> they not?'

In order to establish whether the Devil did have a hand in the affair of *The Hound of the Baskervilles*, Conan Doyle compels Holmes to spend night after night on the moor hiding out in an abandoned stone hut. The author would have seen plenty of these hovels on his expeditions around Dartmoor – they date from the relatively brief period when tin mining flourished in the area. There were indeed two tinners' huts marked on the map close to where I had pitched my tent, but I failed to locate either. Assuming the pixies had not hidden them from me in some knavish jape,

I can only conclude that they had finally succumbed to the elements – which are notoriously unforgiving in these parts – and crumbled away into the sod, footings and all.

The disappearance of the huts was a reminder, if I needed it, that I could expect no help from any outside agency, whether fictional or real, in an emergency. I could not even ring for assistance. I'm not a fan of wireless telephony but I had dug my antiquated mobile from its hideout at the back of a cupboard and brought it along. This was principally to ward off the chidings of friends should something untoward happen to me out in the wilds that I might have been able to set right with a phone call. I noted with grim satisfaction that there was no signal at Wistman's Wood. There hadn't been a signal back at the car park at which I'd left my bicycle either. For all I knew, I had been out of reach of the wider world even as I pedalled through Princetown on my way here. I was truly on my own tonight – a thought that, if I'm honest, rather appealed. After all, what was the worst that could happen?

If one believes the legends about the Devil and his Wisht Hounds, the worst that could happen was that I would be chased from here to a particular hillside 10 miles to the southwest. In my blind terror I would rush straight onto the highest of the Dewerstone crags, known as the Devil's Rock, and topple 150ft to my death. The soundtrack accompanying my three-second fall would be a hellish mixture of thunder claps, the baying of hounds and mirthless laughter. The last sight my eyes would register in this world would be the eerie flutter of brilliant blue flames. The following morning some ill-starred hiker marching through the gorge would come upon my broken body and gape aghast at my features frozen in a look of abject horror (officially the highest degree of horror to which any human can aspire). If, on the other hand, I got lucky and I saw the Devil and his hounds without them seeing me, I would merely die within the year.

One winter night long ago, a man out walking on the moor is said to have heard screams coming from the Dewerstone. Showing an admirable disregard for his own safety, he climbed to the top of the rock and peered over the cliff edge. Down below, the snow had turned dark with blood, the cause of which was only too apparent: the Wisht Hounds were feasting on a human body. The man left the scene at some speed, not daring to stop or look behind him until he was safely home. The next morning, when night's spell was safely broken, he corralled a few friends into going to the Dewerstone to investigate. At the cliff edge they discovered a human footprint in the snow with the impression of a hoof close by. However, there was not a sign of the unfortunate victim of the previous night – all the party found were bloodstains and a lacerated cloak.

Regrettably, the Devil doesn't confine himself to the Dewerstone when finishing off human prey. A popular tale whose setting is usually given as Shaugh Prior or Widecombe sees a moorman returning home from an evening at an inn only to see the Dewer on his headless charger surrounded by his pack of faithful Wisht Hounds. No doubt emboldened by drink, the man calls out to the Devil, asking whether he has had good sport. Laughing, the Devil says that he has. Generous to a fault, the Prince of Darkness tells the man that he is welcome to the kill and throws him a small bundle. The man catches it and takes it home, pleased that he and his young family will have the meat of some animal to cook the next day. On arriving home he and his wife unwrap the package and are distressed to find themselves staring down at the lifeless body of their young child.

The issue of how the Devil stole the infant from the house without its mother noticing is not addressed. The key point is that the child in question was unbaptised, thus making it irresistible to the Devil who, by killing it, would instantly consign it to an eternity in hell. As such, the story served as a morality tale. It clearly suited the Church not to suppress such accounts.

Pondering these gentle histories, the witching hour came near and with it the moment of truth. I lay on the grass with the air hanging around me, heavy and still. Not a sound disturbed the night save the trickle and truckle of my two waterways, now seeming to chuckle together at some private joke. Perhaps they had seen the Devil ride out so often they found him ridiculous. The woods, a black smudge on a Stygian canvas, stirred to action only when my eyes became so mesmerised by staring into the gloom that it danced around before them. It was accompanied by an array of little white dots that would not rest. It suddenly grew discernibly colder and I pulled my coat tighter around me.

I do not remember closing my eyes. Drawn in by the blissful stillness of the night and the downy softness of the air, my body had embraced that little death which is sleep.

When I awoke from a dreamless nap an hour later, Wistman's Wood had vanished. A fog had slithered its way down into the valley and reduced my world to a few strides in any direction. I was all alone but for the company of two large black slugs taking their nightly constitutional. If the sly old Devil had ridden out slightly later than the advertised time in order to take advantage of this concealing cloak of pearl, he had not done so with sufficient brio or ballyhoo to awaken me from my snooze. I could only conclude that tonight he had bigger fish to fry elsewhere. The alternative was that, for hundreds of years, Devonians had been fooling themselves into thinking that the architect of all evil had taken physical form and ridden hither and thither about their moor. They had persuaded themselves that he had done so for the sole purpose of destroying the afterlife prospects of the few locals who had chosen to live there. One can only conclude that they thought rather highly of themselves to have believed their little communities merited such close attention.

Cities, surely, would have produced richer pickings than the dismal moor given their denser populations and the reputation for vice and dissipation that such agglomerations enjoy, yet we have no tradition of lurid tales wherein the Devil roams the streets of Manchester or Glasgow busily harvesting souls.

Why, then, did this particular legend take root on Dartmoor and find so many people ready to believe it? One theory advanced is that travellers across the moor might have reported seeing the Dewer and his pack of unfeasibly fractious hounds when all they had in fact encountered were jack-o'-lanterns. Also known as will-o'-the-wisp, or more prosaically *Ignis fatuus*, these are not the carved Hallowe'en pumpkins that have stolen the name but ethereal lights that are wont to appear at night over marsh and bogs and are often reported to disappear when approached. Science has yet to offer a satisfactory explanation for them, with theories ranging from the natural chemiluminescence of the toxic gas phosphine to electrical currents being produced by quartz beneath the soil. Moonlight, variously bouncing off the caps of honey fungus or the wings of barn owls, has also been posited as a possible source of the phantasmal lights. Whatever their genesis, it's easy to see how the imagination of nocturnal wanderers, already heightened by what the darkness concealed, might transform these jack-o'-lanterns into the red glaring eyes of the hounds, particularly after a pint or two of scrumpy at a local inn.

Then there are the red deer. These majestic creatures roamed Dartmoor in some numbers until 1780 when sheep farmers called upon the Duke of Bedford to eradicate them. His campaign of extermination was so effective that by the time it was over only a few brave and secretive souls were left. In the years that followed, could the unexpected sight of a pair of antlers in the starlight have been taken for the Dewer's horns? One story tells of a sheep farmer who one winter thought he had spotted the Devil in the crepuscular light on Taw Marsh, his horns showing proud of a river bank. As is customary in such tales, the following morning he gathered together a party of friends and returned to the spot to investigate. All they found was a stag caught in the ice at the edge of a river. The Devil apparent had frozen to death.

I saw no antlers or horns, even when the fog began to lift a little and I was able again to pick out the special darkness of Wistman's Wood. There was nothing that might have suggested the glowing red eyes of hounds either. All I had to fire my imagination as the night crawled by were motionless blobs of white that peppered the slopes beyond my tiny river. Had I not noticed a few sheep in the distance earlier in the evening, I might have wondered at these for a while. If they had made any noise as I slept they were silent now. The birds, what few there had been, were evidently dozing somewhere too. All that was left were the mechanical noises of nature – the wind, blowing down some unseen valley a way off, and the water, truckling before and behind me like an aural moat to my guy-roped castle. Wistman's Wood sat sullen and lumpen. There was not even enough of a breeze passing through its clawed branches to whistle me a sinister lullaby.

I lay down on the grass and closed my eyes and let the darkness and the soft night air – now warmer again – enfold me. The night had proved no more evil here than I knew it to be anywhere else. There are many ways of dying after dark out on Dartmoor, but I sank into unconsciousness safe in the knowledge that 'death by encounter with the Devil and his Wisht Hounds' was not one that the rescue services would have to warn against any time soon.

2

Island

If the archaeologists have got it right, there were women and men chipping away at stones and building themselves huts, marking out fields, constructing cairns and possibly even fashioning tiny dams to create freshwater pools on Skomer for thousands of years. The settlement on the tiny island was founded in the dying days of the Stone Age, 5,000 years ago, and continued right through the Bronze Age to very near the end of the Iron Age. The remains from this last era are among the best preserved in the whole of Europe, which explains why most of the isle has been designated a Scheduled Ancient Monument. The struggle for survival that lasted all those years is one that is still played out on the island today, albeit that it's no longer humans that are caught up in it but seabirds, and one rather endearing seabird in particular: the Manx shearwater.

Landing on Skomer at North Haven and climbing the many flights of steps up the cliffs there's an immediate sense of the island having been home to an ancient community. You don't need to be a mystic to perceive this – very close to the landing place there's a large upright menhir called the Harold Stone. As with all the best monoliths, no one is quite sure why it was put there. It may have marked a burial site or had some as yet unfathomed ritualistic significance. Alternatively, it may just have served as a beacon guiding boats into safe harbour. Whatever its purpose, today it enjoys a grandstand view of one of the greatest ornithological events in the British calendar: the nocturnal feeding of the Manx shearwater chicks.

In case this has not got your pulse racing, it should be pointed out that this is no ordinary avian catering operation, for Skomer is home to between 500,000 and 1,000,000 Manx shearwaters, each one in its own burrow and each one waiting to be fed. To complicate matters, their parents must seek the cover of night before running the gauntlet of thousands of predatory gulls to visit the one chick each pair brings into existence every 12 months. If this were not enough, Manx shearwaters are not nocturnal birds. They have no better eyesight than you or I. To increase their chances of outwitting the gulls, they like the night to be as dark and the weather as dirty as possible. They fly in at an incredibly swift 30mph but every second they spend on the ground is charged with the danger of imminent dispatch by a gull. On nights in which there is only a small window of opportunity to visit the island in darkness, they may all attempt to land at roughly the same time, all crying out in tuneless repetitive squawks. It is perhaps not unreasonable, given these conditions, that a state of mayhem ensues.

In early August I took the first of the morning boats over from Martin's Haven, a remote outpost of a far-flung peninsula in the southwest corner of Wales whose existence is indicated only by a tiny jetty and a National Trust car park. Such is the inhospitable nature of Skomer's rocky coastline that North Haven is the sole landing place on the 730-acre island. Despite its name (derived because it lies to the north of a neck of land), North Haven is actually located on the eastern side of Skomer, the only flank not exposed to the full rigours of the Irish Sea. Even with this sheltered natural harbour to aim for, the boat provides something of a fragile link with the mainland. I had booked myself in for two nights on the island but was shipped off after just one because Hurricane Bertha was making its way across the Atlantic. Despite the fact that the storm was weakening with every mile of sea it crossed, the boat was being taken out of the water for five days as a precaution.

I was therefore determined to make the most of my truncated stay and spent nearly the whole day rambling around, looking at everything, and soaking up the sunshine. It's a 4-mile walk on the footpath that runs more or less around the outer edge of Skomer. Add in the other paths that radiate out from the middle of the island, where a ruined farmhouse and converted barn provide it with its human heart, and there's plenty to fill a day. That's especially true if you foster even a passing interest in birds, for Skomer is one squealing, squawking, flapping, scrapping, biffing, whiffling, ululating, mating, pulsating mass of avian life.

The island's resident guillemots and razorbills had upped and gone but I saw fulmars, Northern gannets, cormorants and shags flying hither and thither around the cliffs or standing guard on one of the numerous islets and rocky outcrops that pepper the coast. I also spotted a raft of a dozen or so Atlantic puffins bobbing about just offshore. I have a particular fondness for the Atlantic puffin. Sitting with them is the land-based equivalent of swimming with dolphins when it comes to getting the endorphins flowing and I had been hoping to see many more. Disappointingly, I was informed on the boat coming over that I had missed the vast bulk of them: around 10,000 had left the island just a few days beforehand.

There was still much to enjoy though. I witnessed a couple of nonplussed Canada geese strolling about warily, clearly wishing they had chosen to land in a city park where they had only small children and dogs to contend with. I came within five yards of a raven. He stood so still I thought he was a very realistic statue and was somewhat startled when he suddenly

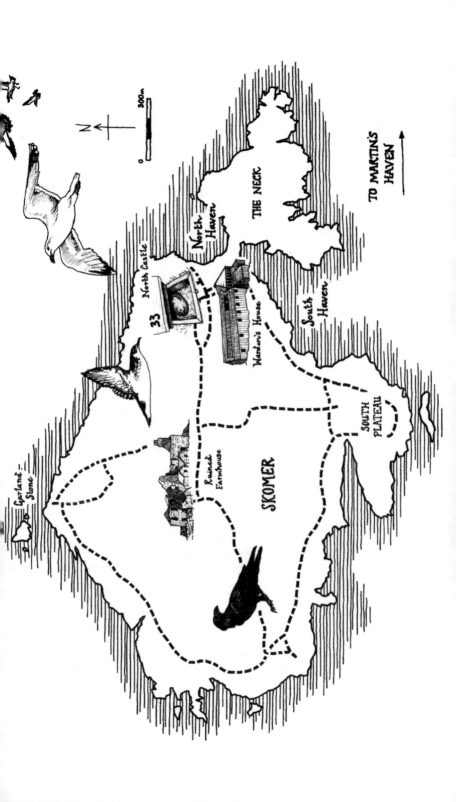

took flight. Not only did he show no fear of me, he downright refused to acknowledge the possibility of my existence.

But more than any of these, I saw gulls. Gulls in their thousands, spearing the ice blue skies with their shrieks and sarcastic laughter. Kittiwakes, lesser black-backed gulls, herring gulls and, the daddy of them all – indeed the largest gull in the world and the shearwater's most fearsome persecutor – the great black-backed gull. I watched them intermingling, colonising a rock here, flying off in a great whirling, scrabbling, ear-splitting flock to patrol the sky, dropping down as one to command a patch of open ground there, pushing off out to sea only to wheel en masse to seize control of another rock, scattering smaller birds like blown confetti. At one point a platoon of great black-backed gulls broke off to circle above me as if I was some kind of trawler. Though their numbers are very low in comparison with the island's other gulls, they make up for it with their sheer size. They have bodies that can measure up to 31 inches and a wingspan that can be twice that length or more.

It was very obvious why the much smaller Manx shearwater, a naturally diurnal bird, would choose to stay far out at sea during the day and only hazard a visit to the island at night. Even then it might not attempt a landing in bright moonlight or starlight. A new moon, coupled with wind and rain, were the conditions shearwaters favoured, no matter if they could hardly see to land themselves.

Even so, as I ambled around the island I found the path strewn with the bodies of shearwaters. Or rather strewn with their heads and legs and feathers, for in most cases the bodies had been devoured. I was told later that the gulls would often not even eat the whole body, preferring to restrict themselves to the choicest parts in the certain knowledge that another ready meal would be along very shortly.

Treeless, and submerged beneath a wash of bracken to the north and east, Skomer is a land of many parts, despite its diminutive size. Just when I thought I had seen the entire island, I came over a ridge to discover swathes of unexplored territory with its own inlets and inclines and cliffs and secretive valleys and yet more burrows. Rabbits were introduced to the island in the 13th century as a food source and both brown and black varieties live here, periodically suffering near extermination thanks to myxomatosis. They are responsible for a good proportion of the million or so burrows, sometimes finding themselves either evicted from them by Manx shearwaters or having the upper chambers taken over by puffins, when the birds can't be bothered to dig for themselves. Their continual grazing also has a dramatic impact on the island's flora. It is only their distaste for bracken that allows that plant to make such hay in the north and east, and I was informed that the island is awash with bluebells in the spring but, as a rule, only the hardiest plants survive the rabbits' busy teeth. I saw sea campion though, and the florid pink of red campion here and there. The thrift was no longer in flower but there was heather and great was my joy in coming across the largest expanse of chamomile I think I've ever seen. This was the plant chosen by Tudor gentry to create the first ever lawns. Its heady scent and copious flowers – a mass of tiny fried eggs waving about in the breeze – make our modern lawns seem rather insipid by comparison.

But despite all this, Skomer is what the Welsh call *moel*: bald. Only the bracken provides any cover for the rabbits and their kits. The Skomer vole – a species unique to the island – also finds some respite there from the attentions of the short-eared owl. However, the vast majority of burrows are blithely exposed to view, offering nothing to protect the Manx shearwater from the gimlet eye of the eternally circling gull.

The only manmade structures that offer any hint of security are dry-stone walls. Farming on the island petered out around 1950, after all but coming to a halt on the outbreak of World War I. Cows, sheep and horses were all grazed here and the long straight walls that once surrounded arable fields near the ruined farmhouse are still standing. It is the prehistoric walls that are the more impressive though, and not simply because of their immense age. For a start, they are built of stones far larger than their more modern counterparts. To look at any one of them is to feel the back-breaking toil that must have gone into creating them. They are also wide, soul-destroyingly wide when the wall must stretch so very far and life is so very very brief. Thirty-five was a maturity few would obtain, even in the sophisticated Iron Age.

I have descended into a 5,000-year-old burial cairn and walked among the ruins of a Bronze Age village but neither made me feel an affinity with my prehistoric ancestors like these structures. There's something in the straightforwardness of a dry-stone wall that transcends the millennia: it is built in a certain immediately comprehensible way and has a certain unambiguous purpose that has not changed in all the years since those early inhabitants of Skomer sweated these stones into position. Our burial places are not like their burial places, our houses are not like their houses, but we still build dry-stone walls, even in an age when we can send a probe into space and land it on a comet.

I couldn't help but think that the steadfastly primeval character of the island made it a fitting amphitheatre for the nightly drama played out around its shores each summer. The themes it touched upon were, after all, pretty much timeless: the precarious nature of existence; parents risking everything for their offspring; the weak and vulnerable battling to outwit the strong and predatory; the death of one sustaining the life of another.

At Night

I had carelessly chosen to visit about a week before a full moon but, as the afternoon progressed, the sky became overcast and so my hopes of a dark and perhaps even stormy night increased. Heartened by this, at eight o'clock I attended the daily log at which volunteers gather around a kitchen table to report the species of birds and other creatures they have observed during the day. This evening's big news was of a possible large raptor on the island. There had been no confirmed sighting but something had been putting the wind up the gulls and, since one of the volunteers described having seen a bird that resembled 'a gigantic sparrowhawk', a goshawk was thought the most likely culprit. I smiled at this. I hadn't yet seen a single one of Skomer's Manx shearwaters – not a living one at any rate – but I already felt enough of a kinship with them to consider my friends' enemies' enemy to be my friend. Also, having once gone eyeball to eyeball with a sparrowhawk while sitting in my flat in London – a startling 15-second encounter that had burnt itself onto my brain – the thought of 'a gigantic sparrowhawk' stalking the island was rather exciting.

As night drew on, one of the affable wardens on Skomer introduced me to Ollie, a young Oxford academic from Merseyside who was living on the island in order to carry out research on Manx shearwaters, or 'Manxies' as I soon learned to call them. He dazzled me with tales of his investigations into these unostentatious birds with their plain black uppers and their plain white undercarriages. He then cruelly swore me to secrecy about them until he had published his findings. Happily, there is a great deal we already know about this modest yet rather astounding little seabird that can be shared. Not for nothing, it seems, is the collective noun for shearwaters an 'improbability'.

Puffinus puffinus, to give the Manx shearwater its scientific name (confusingly, the Atlantic puffin is *Fratercula arctica*), is a member of the same order of birds as the Ancient Mariner's albatross, a group once called tubenoses but now known rather more decorously as petrels. It owes its English name to the fact that the biggest colony in the world once lived on the Isle of Man. Unfortunately, the colony was all but annihilated by rats that swam ashore after a shipwreck in the 18th century, which is perhaps another reason why no one on Man may speak that rodent's name. The planet's largest concentration of Manx shearwaters can now be found on Skomer, an island without rats. According to Ollie, this insubstantial droplet of land off the Marloes Peninsula is home to about half the world's population of Manx shearwaters, doubtless drawn here by soil soft enough for the digging of burrows, the plentiful supply of ready-made ones, easy access to the sea and relative lack of human activity (visitors to Skomer are strictly counselled to keep to footpaths to avoid putting their feet through burrows). It's just a pity about the gulls.

However, the remarkable thing about Manxies is not that they live on Skomer but what they do each year from September to February when they are *not* on Skomer. For a start, they like to over-winter in Argentina – I suspect a lot of us would, if given the chance – so they set off initially for West Africa and the Canaries before crossing the Atlantic. It's a journey of roughly 7,000 miles and the record for a tagged shearwater is around 156 hours – an average speed of 44mph. That's quite a lick for a bird whose body you can hold fairly comfortably in one hand and whose wingspan is between 30 and 35 inches.

Furthermore, this outward trip accounts for less than half of their annual journey. When they decide to up sticks and return to Europe, Manxies fly north to the United States, up that country's eastern seaboard, across to Iceland and then down to Wales, clocking up another 9–10,000 miles. This may seem (indeed, it is) a circuitous way of getting back to their burrows on Skomer but there's a method to the apparent madness. For very large parts of their grand tour, the shearwaters cadge a lift on trade winds. The only section in which they have to struggle against the prevailing winds is from Argentina up to North America.

This canny utilisation of the winds is not the only ace they have up their wing coverts.

'They use a technique called sheer soaring,' Ollie explained, 'which is where they use the air currents coming up off the waves. They go just along the top of them and so fly terribly efficiently. They're incredibly inefficient at low speed flight though. And you'll see them on land tonight where they're just…'

He paused, searching for the precise ornithological term that would sum up their prowess as pedestrians: '…useless.'

We laughed and adjourned to wander behind the ruined farmhouse where some other researchers were taking time off to peer through a telescope at the night sky.

Viewing the stars and planets was something of a bittersweet experience. I felt the warm glow of having witnessed some very special sights but, at the same time, the fact that so much of the heavens could be seen boded ill for my night among the Manxies, which was, after all, why I had come to Skomer. Ollie sized up the disturbing number of lumens pouring out of the night sky and suggested we leave it until 3am before meeting up, on the grounds that it was unlikely to get dark enough for the shearwaters to risk landing before then. One of his fellow researchers was leaving the island the next day so he went off to drink his health, having given me thorough instructions as to where we would reconvene in four hours' time. Neither feeling tired nor relishing the thought of going to sleep only to be ripped from my dreams in the middle of the night, I sauntered off down the wide grassy track away from the hostel and the soft chatter of people whose isolated existence had drawn the bonds of friendship all the tighter, and headed slowly out towards North Haven, half a mile away. The air wrapped itself around my face like a warm flannel. Up ahead, roughly in the direction of the meeting place, herring gulls and lesser black-backed gulls were making a racket.

By 1.45am the cacophony had not subsided by a single decibel. I had recklessly assumed that they would grow quieter at night but I realised I had a lot to learn about birds and their sleeping habits. I should have known better really. One snowy January I persuaded a friend that a certain remote and lissome valley in the Peak District would be an excellent spot to camp for the night despite the fact that, when we arrived, there was an almighty din coming from a rookery on the far bank of the stream we had followed in.

'Don't worry, they'll all be asleep by midnight,' I had blithely assured him with the confidence of A Man Who Knew Rooks. At three o'clock, without a wink of sleep between us, I acknowledged that they might never actually drop off. I was mistaken in that assertion too because at seven, when we finally gave it up as a bad job and emerged from our tents, they fell silent. Perhaps they felt their work was done. We certainly haven't returned.

Now, standing near North Castle, a rock that marks the northeast corner of the island, I was immersed in the prattling of hundreds of gulls. No, wait — that does not really do them justice. It was not mere prattling. The noise was more akin to a huge gang of gulls all rolling drunk out of the pubs at closing time and proceeding to scream and shout at each other with the sort of abandon that only a liverful of strong continental lager can impart. No Manx shearwater in its right mind would walk into that. Furthermore, the moon was slightly more than three-quarters full and unpromisingly brilliant even when the odd cloud passed before it. My only hope was that the leading edge of whatever was left of Hurricane Bertha arrived before dawn.

Beyond the fracas there was a tanker at anchor. It was so brightly lit that to anyone gazing in Earth's direction from another planet it must have seemed like a whole new star had materialised out of nowhere. Disconcertingly, it also appeared to have an intercontinental ballistic missile slung across it. When I asked Ollie about the ship later he confessed that he too was at a loss as to why it had to dazzle so. There were sometimes three or four of them parked in the bay and he pondered whether some Manxies might be blinded by their lights and crash into them. (He thought the missile was probably just a large crane though.) On the mainland, three towers of bright red lights revealed the location of oil refineries at Milford Haven, adding yet more light and confusion to the scene. Everything seemed to militate against the safe passage of the Manxie. Surely the act of feeding your only child shouldn't be this hard? It made me wonder why they hadn't decamped en masse to some darker corner of the coast that was perhaps less gull-friendly into the bargain.

I ambled back disconsolately towards the hostel. In the moonlight, the ruined farmhouse opposite looked ghoulish, as if it had been torn from the cover of a cheap 1950s horror novel. It was an impression that was enhanced by the gulls who swooped around me at close quarters and who looked like black ghosts. When they flew across the moon the phantoms transformed themselves into huge vampire bats. If Bram Stoker had come here instead of Whitby, I've no doubt he would still have been inspired to write *Dracula*.

Above the farmhouse huge Gainsborough clouds began to accumulate – immense cumulus affairs with dark underbellies full not of rain but shadows. At last, true darkness had arrived. But no sooner had I had the thought than the clouds parted, moonlight poured out through the gap like a searchlight and I was caught in its beam, a prisoner of war escaping over the wire.

When three o'clock comes I'm standing at the spot designated by Ollie. The bay that serves as the island's harbour lies before me. The sea far below glistens here and there in the moonlight. All around me an untidy sprawl of burrows spreads out as far as I can see. Towards the cliffs, a light snaps on in a window of the island office, a large wooden building overlooking the bay. A minute later Ollie joins me. He has the fresh face of a man whose body clock has long since accustomed itself to consciousness at this hour. For my part, I've passed through the slightly tipsy feeling that comes upon me when I'm battling sleep and I'm now very much awake. The fact that I have seen my first, second and third Manx shearwaters of the night is also proving more of a stimulus than could any amount of caffeine.

I heard the Manxies before I saw them. The gulls had, for the time being, decided to confine their operations to North Castle, a few hundred yards away on the far side of the Harold Stone, and although they were still creating something of a commotion, the urgent rasping awk-awk-aaaaww of the shearwaters, just a matter of yards from my head, cut through the tumult. The moon, sadly, had shown no sign of dimming, so these first arrivals of the night were the ones Ollie had described to me earlier as either being so desperate to feed their chick that they ignored the danger or those who had 'some other agenda'. I was charmed at the idea of Manxies having an agenda. Indeed, it was clearly so sophisticated a bird that it even went so far as entertaining some agenda that was not its normal one.

While we wait for things to pick up, I ask Ollie why I've seen so many dead shearwaters on the paths around the island and not a single corpse belonging to any of the other smaller species of birds, of which there are many on Skomer.

The answer is a combination of mathematics and design. 'There are more Manx shearwaters on the island than anything else by one or maybe two orders of magnitude,' he tells me in an accent not quite Scouse but not quite anything else, 'but the main reason is they're just easy prey. If you ever see one on the ground you'll see why – they're just very, very vulnerable. Their legs are really far back on their body, which means they can't take off very easily. They're also really clumsy, which doesn't help. When they take off they run downhill flapping frantically and eventually become airborne. But if a gull gets them before they do...'

A scene of violence and devastation rises before my eyes.

'If they come out of their burrows late or if they don't leave before it's light and a gull gets it on the ground then it's got no chance. However, if the Manxie gets fully airborne then it can outfly almost anything.'

Ollie shows me the study burrows used by the research group of which he's a member. They have been slightly excavated and then, to ensure that the chick inside is safe from harassment from gulls but still accessible to its smaller, nimbler parents, a paving slab has been placed on top. I have seen such study burrows all over the island but Ollie has his hundred here where they are close to hand. Each one has a marker with a hand-painted number on it. Ollie reaches down into burrow 33.

Like a magician pulling a rabbit from a hat, he withdraws his arm and there in his hand is something for which I am completely unprepared. It is a slightly larger and slightly fluffier version of the windshield on my sound recorder, and exactly the same shade of mid-grey. So striking is the similarity that were we now to put the windshield into the burrow instead of the chick I can imagine it being fed by the parents for weeks before they got wise to the subterfuge.

Ollie hands the chick to me and my heart melts, for who can resist a vulnerable little bundle of fluff whose own heart is pitter-pattering away inside? I'm shown how to hold the chick gently – with one hand around the back to keep its wings closed and the other underneath the feet to support it. That mastered, I put all my ornithological skills into determining where its head is. Unfortunately, it's so fluffy that it's impossible to tell. Ollie tells me, perhaps in an attempt to console, that it's also impossible to determine its sex at this stage too. But its head? I scan up and down to find any distinguishing features at either end but, no, I'm holding a ball of bubbles. It's just after 3am on a little island off the Pembrokeshire coast and I'm kneeling down on the grass cradling a Manx shearwater chick. Sitting out at sea somewhere, one or both of its parents are almost certainly eyeing the sky with increasing alarm, full of sand eels to regurgitate into their offspring's waiting bill but stymied by a moon that stubbornly refuses to hide itself away.

The chick doesn't appear at all distressed at being held, which was my main concern when Ollie suggested we take one out to look at it. I can't even be sure that it's woken up. All things considered, it's commendably unfazed by the whole experience – I think if a giant hand had grabbed me and pulled me from my bed, I'd be trying to do something about it by now. Looking down at the peaceful little mite I feel a surge of happiness welling up within me. I'm sure this is not how proper naturalists react but I don't really care. Indeed, Ollie seems almost as thrilled by the chick as I am and he must have held them innumerable times. Eventually, the fluff begins to cheep, the sort of squeaking sound you get if you rub a balloon up and down a window. It evidently thinks this disturbance is its mum or dad coming with food. It means I can also see its bill at last. It is almost black and rather wide with two pronounced slits in the top and a downward hook at the end.

On the appearance of the bill, Ollie points out the importance of our bird's olfactory bulb. 'It's probably crucial when it comes to navigation. Manxies don't have large brains but they do lots of smelling – they're very sensitive to microscopic changes in odour concentration.' He tells me of an experiment carried out in the Azores with some Cory's shearwaters, a similar but larger species. Half of the group had their sense of smell blocked before they were released 500 miles offshore. 'The ones that couldn't smell just wandered around randomly. The ones that could got straight home.'

Our chick isn't quite ready for flight yet but will be so in roughly four weeks from now. It needs to put a bit of weight on first though and lose the down on its wings. Unusually, Manx shearwater chicks actually get larger than the adults before they fledge. An adult will weigh about 14oz but the chicks can grow as heavy as 25oz. Once they're good and plump, their parents abandon them. Over the next eight days or so the unfed chicks lose weight and become hungry, which is a stimulus to get them to leave their burrows and see something of the world. Some of those extra reserves are used to grow the feathers that our downy urchin still lacks.

'They go quite quickly from being a big ball of fluff to looking all feathered and ready to go,' Ollie adds. 'He doesn't look like he's ready to go to Argentina in a month's time, does he?'

And I have to confess that he (or just as possibly she) doesn't. In fact, even to suggest that this mewling dependent little thing will start a journey of 7,000 miles next month, crossing the world's second largest ocean, seems an act of enormous faith or simple lunacy.

What is perhaps even more astonishing is that if this chick manages to avoid the less than tender mercies of the gulls when it leaves the burrow, it may well go on to live to a grand old age. Far from sending the Manx shearwater to an early grave, its annual 17,000-mile odyssey evidently fortifies it.

'The record is about 51 years,' Ollie tells me. The champion is a bird that was tagged as an adult nearly half a century ago and lives on Skokholm, an island just a hop and a skip along the coast from here. 'But if you think of what a small proportion are ringed and what a small proportion of those are re-trapped, the chances are that the 51-year-old isn't the oldest but just the oldest that we know about.'

Imagine that – travelling under your own steam from Britain to Africa to South America to North America to Iceland and back to Britain every year of your life for more than 50 years. Include the other journeys it must undertake in order to feed and mate and go about the business of survival and this insubstantial bird will have flown well in excess of a million miles in its lifetime. You have to take your hat off to that.

'The chicks that we see here now are going to outlive us,' Ollie declares with what I detect is a trace of triumph in his voice, for these are his babies too. Tortoises notwithstanding, one usually imagines that one will see out any animals one comes across. That some of these fragile little things lurking beneath the ground may still be soaring across the Atlantic years after I have left the stage is a sobering thought. At least it's a sobering thought until I gently remind myself that nature isn't necessarily all about me.

I return Chick 33 to Ollie. He places it safely into its burrow and puts the slab back in place. More birds are beginning to come in now. It's likely that they've calculated that with dawn just a couple of hours away this is as dark as it's going to get tonight so they're plucking up their courage and risking it. There are no gulls that I can see in the immediate vicinity so the Manxies around us are probably safe enough. It's fortunate for them that gulls are equally ill-equipped for night-time manoeuvres, which means that both parties end up blundering about.

The awk-awk-aaaaww, which sounds like every Manxie on the island has contracted a horribly sore throat that they're trying desperately to clear, now comes from in front of us and behind us, to our left and to our right, above our heads and down by our feet. However, the purpose behind this call remains a mystery. According to Ollie, there's no shortage of theories about males and females recognising each other by them. 'People in the 20th century' – the way he says this makes it sound like the days of Queen *Victoria* – 'thought that they might echolocate. We know that's not true. It's probably some sort of sexual selection or partner calling. Frankly, it would be much easier to find out if you could actually see them.'

At Night

Tonight may be a poor one in terms of sheer numbers of Manxies but wherever I look I can see them emerging as if from nowhere only to disappear again out to sea, their black upper parts still an effective camouflage in spite of the moonlight. Each flying visit lasts only as long as it takes for the bird to enter the burrow, feed the chick and get airborne again – a matter of minutes. Though we've had some near misses, none have crashed into us yet. Counter-intuitively, the fact that Ollie and I are both wearing dark clothing means we're less likely to be struck. If we were to shine a torch, the shearwaters would be dazzled and fly straight at the source of the light.

The birds that race past us in a flap will have flown huge distances of late in addition to their annual migration. Ollie tells me that GPS devices placed on some of the Manxies during incubation show that most fly up to the waters off southwest Ireland or the Isle of Man to feed. Others prefer the Hebrides while one adventurous soul went almost as far as Iceland – a 1,200-mile round trip.

'Do they ever sleep?' I ask, somewhat in awe of this perpetual motion, 'because they're clearly not catching 40 winks in the burrows.'

They do, apparently – mainly out at sea at night, when they're not keeping an eye on the moon or haring off to Skomer to feed their chick. They also have a chance to get some kip during incubation, which is a shared effort between the parents. One will sit on the egg for up to a fortnight at a time while their partner forages. Then they'll swap round. The bird doing the egg-sitting goes hungry all the while it's in the burrow, which explains why they are prepared to travel such long distances in search of a good feed.

Towards 4am, with the maddening moon still beaming down on us, we wander to the island office so that Ollie can make us cups of tea. We chat about his researches; why American songbirds are so often the preferred choice of the avian researcher (it's largely down to practicalities); and whether Manx shearwaters, like some American songbirds, use the Earth's magnetic fields to navigate (it doesn't appear that they do).

When we emerge, I have the feeling that it is perhaps a tiny bit darker outside. With hindsight I suspect this is wishful thinking combined with a loss of night vision caused by the brightly lit kitchen. I put my tea down on a picnic table and we watch as more Manxies career in off the sea, landing with a modest 'thunk' next to their burrows. 'On a really dark night, when they all come in, you can hear them crash into the building – thud, thud, thud,' Ollie informs me, sounding like a survivor from Hitchcock's *The Birds*. I wince, but apparently they usually pick themselves up and carry on about their business. Earlier, we saw one bird go full pelt into the substantial bench next to where we met up. I was sure it had either killed itself or at the very least broken a wing. However, after a few dazed strides it came to its senses and darted off towards a burrow. They also contrive to crash into each other on the wing. 'You'd imagine it was a rare event but I hear it pretty much every night,' Ollie says. 'I've seen them hit each other and one just falls down and dies.'

With this my companion suggests we walk up the path to a denser part of the colony. The next few seconds are logged for posterity, captured on my digital recorder with its chick-covered microphone:

'Feel free to bring your tea,' Ollie says.

Boof!

It's the unmistakable sound of Manx shearwater hitting waterproof jacket. A bird has caught me smack in the middle of my right shoulder blade at about 30mph.

'Their sensory systems aren't fantastic,' says Ollie, displaying a laudable commitment to understatement.

'That was very odd,' I reply. 'Normally when you get hit by something you cry out, but on this occasion my brain immediately kicked in with "Oh, that's perfectly natural." It was as if I got hit in the back by a Manx shearwater every day.' I didn't even spill my tea, my proudest achievement for some while.

It seems I got off lightly. As we walk up the path, Ollie recounts the tale of a master's student carrying out research on the island who got hit on the forehead by a Manxie. His glasses were broken and his face was cut open. By contrast, my little mishap didn't even leave a bruise.

'I'm glad that's happened,' Ollie says cheerfully, 'because you may not have had the best night for it but at least you've been hit by a Manxie.'

Back at the spot by the bench where we had met up, the shearwaters are using the path as a makeshift runway. Their legs are indeed absurdly far back on their bodies. This is very helpful when propelling themselves through water and they are excellent swimmers, but on the ground they are, as Ollie had pointed out, useless. To become airborne they either need to get up quite a bit of speed or climb up onto something, throw themselves off and flap wildly. Furthermore, they are hampered by their slender wings, which, although long and very efficient for shooting mile after mile across the tops of waves, do not give them very much initial lift. A headwind can help them get aloft but tonight what little wind there is blows from the land behind us, making conditions for take-off very poor indeed.

We watch as birds trundle along the path towards the sea, lift themselves off the ground through much frenzied fluttering and then come painfully back down to earth a few yards later. One decides to climb a small rock nearby. The summit can't be more than 18 inches higher than the grassy tussocks around it but even so it is gained only after a struggle. At the top the Manxie has a little look around and then hurls itself off, only to come to grief shortly afterwards. Undeterred, it waddles back, awkwardly clambers up the rock and tries again. This time it skims the ground but somehow makes it out to sea and away from danger.

'They'll look for any height advantage they can in order to take off,' Ollie tells me. 'On a good night, if you sit still they just climb all over you.'

The next moment he's standing with an adult shearwater in his hands. I'm invited to stroke the back of its head but it's not having any of that – it whips its bill around and nips me sharply on the finger, which is fair enough really. Ollie places it on my wrist so that I suddenly take on the appearance of a falconer. In order to make amends for my presumption in stroking it, I try to be the best launch pad I can be and begin to raise my arm but the Manxie is barely at head height before it decides it has enough altitude to make a successful take-off. It explodes into the night, drops rather alarmingly towards the grass and paving slabs, then just about produces sufficient propulsion to level out until the ground falls away beneath it and it vanishes into the darkness. I give a cheer, for it's very satisfying to see it succeed. If helping Manx shearwaters to get airborne were something one could make a living at, I'd be dusting off my CV quicker than you can say *Puffinus puffinus*.

I'm also buoyed by the fact that my new friends are not that easy to kill. 'Normally a black-backed gull would need to drown them,' Ollie tells me. 'Manxies have got a really good bite on them' – this I had just discovered – 'they're tough little birds and it's not so easy to snap their necks.'

The newly fledged chicks are a slightly different matter, however. Around 40 to 50 ravens begin to gather on Skomer in mid-August. The statuesque one I had stumbled across earlier in the day had clearly been the vanguard. It meant that the chicks, now safely hidden below us, were even more vulnerable when they emerged than their parents are when feeding them. They could not guarantee a dark and stormy night in which to sneak away, and they had not only the gulls to contend with but hungry ravens too. It cannot be a pleasant thing for the first seconds you ever spend outside your warm cosy burrow to be filled not with the reassuring calls of your parents but with wild eyes you do not know, then flashing bills and grasping claws or slashing talons.

Towards 5am the sky over the mainland lightened with the first hints of dawn. The last of the adult Manx shearwaters panicked themselves into flight. The final cries of awk-awk-aaaaww went rasping their way out to sea. The chicks in their burrows settled down for another day of quiet contemplation, or as quiet as the squabbling gulls above would allow. In this little part of the island at least, the Manxies who had braved the moonlight had all lived to return again tomorrow. Their chicks would be busily digesting the disgorged sand eel and thus putting on weight. This would stand them in good stead for the transformation into fully fledged birds they must make all too soon and increase their own chances of survival when they emerged from their burrows. Tonight, the weak and vulnerable had outfoxed the strong and predatory: we had not seen one of them on our patch give up their own life to sustain the life of a black-backed gull. I felt that any spirits of the ancient inhabitants of Skomer who might be looking on from the Harold Stone would have nodded their approval (while also no doubt speculating about how good a Manx shearwater chick might taste: lightly grilled, perhaps, on a bed of oatmeal gruel). And though I acknowledge that the island's black-backed gulls experience their own day-to-day struggle for existence, I couldn't help feeling pleased that, as far as we knew, they had not filled their bellies with the soft flesh of any of the Manxies around here tonight.

I said goodnight to Ollie and he strode back down to the island office and a welcome bed. After a while I turned back up the footpath, my mind replaying the frantic taxiing and scurrying of the Manxies I had seen use it as a runway. It was now just light enough to make out the Harold Stone, gaunt and impassive and still loyally carrying out whatever duties it had been burdened with so long ago. After all the hustle and bustle of the last couple of hours I felt the primordial character of the island reassert itself.

As I made my way back to my own bed, I heard 'Psssssst! Psssssst!' Somewhere above a sea of bracken to my left a short-eared owl chick was calling out to me that the shearwaters weren't the only show in town here at night. For several hundred yards I heard the cry, sometimes at very close quarters, and I hoped all the time that its owner would break cover. The fact that it did not was disappointing but, I thought, augured well for the life expectancy of the chick.

The last action of the night was provided by a party of great black-backed gulls. Perhaps keen to take out the frustrations of a night of slim pickings on anything that happened to be abroad, they swooped and swirled around, spitting out their gruff kow-kow-kow as if strafing me. I walked on and, in the dawn light, the farmhouse appeared up ahead at last. It had lost its ghoulishness and now fancied itself a castle ruined à la picturesque.

Months later, sitting at home, writing these words on the brink of a British winter, I allow myself the sentimental hope that Chick 33 made it out to sea. I imagine it basking in the sunshine on some Argentinian shore, surrounded by new sights, new sounds and, above all, new smells to keep that outsize olfactory bulb entertained. I also like to think it might have some ingrained atavistic sense that it is extremely fortunate to have been born a Manx shearwater, for it is starting out on what is one of our planet's more extraordinary lives.

3

Forest

I have spent many nights camping in woods. I have listened to the sound of the wind in the treetops, the uncanny hoots of tawny owls and the scurrying about of various wild animals, identified by my imagination as more exotic creatures than, in all likelihood, they were (the only time I was certain that the pootling about I heard outside was a hedgehog was when one decided to set up home under my flysheet). On many of these occasions, I have told myself – from the cosy warmth of my sleeping bag – that I really ought to pass an entire night wandering about among the trees, rather than sharing their nocturnal life at one remove, behind a barrier of rip-stop nylon.

As is the fate of so many of my resolutions, the years slid by while the pledge I had made myself stalked the nether reaches of my mind, making its way to the forefront whenever I camped in or near a wood, only to be chased back into the shadows by life's more pressing commitments. It was, then, a pleasure long overdue to find myself sitting by an immense oak tree one midsummer's eve, waiting for darkness to fall so that I could begin a night's sylvan expedition.

Given the choice of all the many fine forests that still exist in Britain – an island once so densely and comprehensively wooded that it was said a squirrel could travel from one end to the other without touching the ground – I plumped for the most famous of all: Sherwood. I did so partly on a whim. This, of course, was the forest said to have been inhabited by Robin Hood and his Merrie Men, who would have spent hundreds of nights under the woodland's protective canopy. However, there was an additional spur. I have been fortunate enough to visit practically every nook and cranny of this island – either to immortalise them in timeless prose or simply for the pleasure of nosing about – and I was shocked to realise that I had never been to Sherwood Forest.

I would put that right by spending the hours from dusk till dawn roaming hither and thither through some of the vast tracts of woodland that make up the forest. I would experience the double darkness of a night in a wood, where any light of moon or stars must find its way past a thick mantle of leaves if it is to illuminate the floor of the greenwood and those passing along it. I would commune with whatever nocturnal wildlife called this place home. If nothing else, it would make a change to be able to identify the creatures of the wood, rather than speculate whether a particular rustling had been made by an especially light and nimble deer or an especially heavy and clumsy squirrel.

Sherwood has never been a single body of trees but a patchwork of woods interrupted by large areas of scrub or heath. However, it was once rather larger than today's manifestation. When it served as a royal hunting forest it stretched from near Worksop in the north all the way to Nottingham, over 20 miles away to the south; and from Laxton in the east 20 miles to Chesterfield in the west. It is the poor quality soil of the Bunter sandstone on which most of the forest stands that accounts for the generous expanses of heathland that form an integral part of its character.

The trees that have managed to make a go of it on the unpromising terrain are those best adapted to the soil – silver birches, hollies, rowans, hawthorns and, most famously, oaks. The sessile and pedunculate oaks that grow here survive by sending down long tap roots to reach the water table far below. One of their number is the tree most associated with Robin Hood – the Major Oak. Its aged branches supported by a complex network of metal poles, this is purported to be the largest oak in England and thus seemed a fitting starting point for a night among trees. More than likely well over a thousand years old, its Brobdingnagian dimensions meant, of course, that it was ripe for fashioning as the tree used by Robin Hood and his associates as a hideout and sleeping quarters. It's also said that 34 children can get inside the Major Oak's hollow trunk, which seems as good a use to put children to as any, but why it never shared the fate of its contemporaries and fell to the woodman's axe is a mystery we are never likely to solve.

Watching the steadily failing light darken the tree's piteously enfeebled branches, I became aware of a slender fox. He made a wide arc around me, trit-trotting purposefully as he began his nightly rounds. As one of the top predators in the wood he could patrol his territory with some confidence.

I pulled on more clothes as the temperature began to dip, although it remained somewhat humid. This reminded me to catch the weather forecast on the radio I had brought with me. I learnt that a series of thunderstorms heading north from London was due to ravage the country throughout the night. This had not been in my plans. However, I cheered myself up with the thought that Robin Hood and his cohorts would have faced much worse and yet were universally considered to have been merrie, so I too should not let anything as trifling as the weather get me down.

Shortly after ten, dusk turned to night and I set off. My intention was to take in three of Sherwood Forest's principal woods: Birklands, where I was

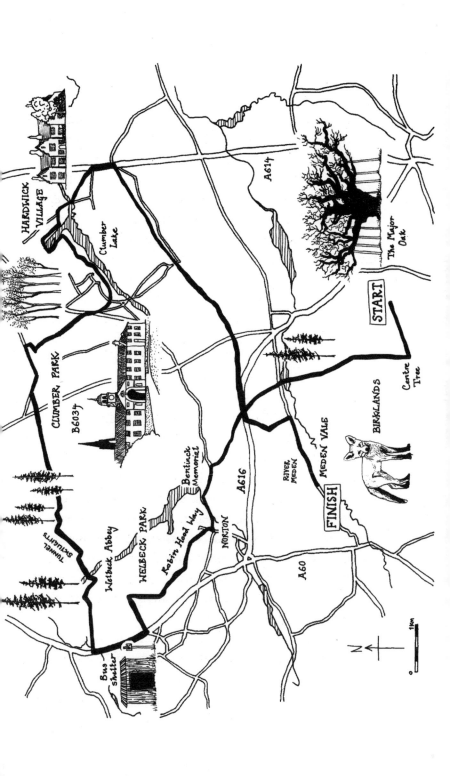

now, Welbeck Park and Clumber Park – the three forming a rough triangle. The latter two are part of The Dukeries, an area comprising no fewer than four contiguous ducal estates. Rather than ride a horse between them, as Robin and his companions would doubtless have done where possible, I would pedal around on my bicycle, largely following the Robin Hood Way, a long-distance footpath which, in these parts, doubles as a cycle path for much of its route.

I struck out west from the Major Oak, a dead straight track that took me to the Centre Tree. As its name suggests, it stands at the core of Birklands, a wood whose own name stems from the birch tree. At about 300 years old, this oak is a comparative youngster and, in oak tree terms, in the prime of life. Unfortunately, it also looks like an ordinary oak tree. Even playing my bike light up and down it in a jazzy manner could not make it appear extraordinary.

I was about to turn north up a rough path when I was struck by a remarkable sound coming from high up in the trees ahead of me.

'Hhhhhhhhhhhhhhhhhhha!'

It was as if someone were tapping out Morse code at such a tremendous lick that they were forgetting to include any dashes. I stood stock still and waited to see if the manic signaller would call again.

'Hhhhhhhhhhhhhhhhhhha!'

'Hhhhhhhhhhhhhhhha!'

The cry burred through the trees. I refined my assessment of it. It was a telegraphist sending Morse code at such extreme speed that it impersonated the tuneless call of the toad, only in a slightly higher register and with occasional changes of pitch. Experienced birders – among whom I do not number myself – will often talk of the 'unmistakable' call of this bird or that but in this case the word is apt, for no other bird sounds quite like the nightjar. It's pretty distinctive to look at too. A funny stubby-looking thing, the nightjar sports disproportionately large buggy eyes – all the better for seeing at night – a short bill concealing a wide moth-gobbling mouth, and a camouflage jacket of mottled brown-and-grey plumage that resembles the bark of the trees in which it sits. Its twin glories are its wings – fine long graceful affairs like those of a raptor – and the Morse/toad call that goes tearing through the woods at night, each little dot a tooth on a saw.

I cycled slowly up the path, now noticing the occasional chirrup that is the male nightjar's other, less distinctive call. A little further along, where one bird was clearly quite close by, I stopped to make a recording. The calls were soon joined by the sound of footsteps coming towards me from somewhere in the darkness.

'It's an unpaired male,' the maker of the footsteps informed me. 'There's a pair further down.'

My interlocutor, it turned out, was an affable chap named Andy from the Nottinghamshire Wildlife Trust who had just come from leading a group of birdwatchers around the forest. Andy had put GPS tags on these particular nightjars so that he and his colleagues could monitor them.

'They're flying up to 9 miles to feed. They breed here and then go up to just past Ollerton.'

I should have been more impressed than I was by that, but now that I knew that Manx shearwaters sometimes flew up to Iceland for a meal, 'just past Ollerton' didn't seem like much of a stretch.

I asked him what else I should be keeping an ear out for.

'There's quite a few long-eared owls. If you listen out for them they sound like a squeaky gate. We just had a fantastic view of one. There are still a few woodlarks about too – they've gone a bit quiet but they'll start singing again soon.'

Now, I can spot a skylark's song from a thousand paces – it basically sounds like that Vaughan Williams' *Lark Ascending* – but I was less sure of myself with regards to the woodlark.

'It repeats itself,' Andy began. It's supposed to say *lu-la*, so it goes *lu-la lu-la lu-la*. It's meant to be the best British birdsong.'

He didn't sound convinced by this.

'I've seen a male tonight sat on a fence but he wasn't singing,' he added with a slightly dismissive air, as if to emphasise his dissident stance on the subject.

He went on to inform me that if I went to Centre Tree I'd see lots of glow-worms in the grass. 'One or two hundred on a good night.'

This caused me a deal of anguish – I had clearly been so occupied with my bike light trying to make the Centre Tree seem interesting that I had missed the show that had doubtless been going on at my feet.

We parted, but not before he had told me that wandering about in Sherwood Forest at night was his life, at least in the summer. There was hardly a night when the weather was decent that he wasn't out and about until the wee small hours. I found this oddly comforting. Here was somebody who, when I explained to him that I would be roaming about the forest all night, didn't think it in the least bit strange. It was pleasant to know too that there might be other night owls like me bumbling about beneath the trees following their own particular passion.

I wondered if perhaps these might include badger watchers or, even better, badgers. A few weeks previously, while walking one night along clifftops in Cornwall, I had encountered three badgers from three different setts. 'The most ancient Briton of English beasts,' as the poet Edward Thomas described them, is the wild creature I love the most. No night in which I come across even one has been a night wasted. I knew there were badgers in Sherwood but interminable hours spent in badger hides have taught me that knowing they are there and actually seeing them are two very different things indeed.

The path became a track inhabited by frogs and, as I neared a road, it left the wood and was carried over the River Meden by a bridge. Now that I had come out from under the trees I saw that there was still a little light left in the sky and grey-orange clouds piling up over to the west. I had listened out for squeaky gates and *lu-la lu-las* but had come up empty-eared, so decided to stop on the bridge to see if I could spot the angular profile of a heron on the bank or perhaps a late-partying grebe out on the water.

Almost immediately there was a splashing directly beneath me that augured well. Then the noise stopped as abruptly as it had begun. I peered down, but whatever had come up onto the bank, about 10ft below me, was lost in the shadow of the bridge.

'Probably a duck,' I surmised, before immediately revising that opinion – the disturbance had clearly been caused by a larger creature. After all, it had been a *splash* or, more correctly, a *splosh*, not a mere *splish*. A goose then. Not a Canada goose, for even in the penumbra of the bridge I should have seen its white neck. A greylag goose perhaps. That would blend entirely into the gloomy surroundings below me if it kept its underparts down. Tired of listening, I did what I suspect no proper naturalist would ever dream of doing. I shone a light roughly towards the place where I had heard the *splosh*. The beam picked out two glowing red eyes looking up at me.

They were not the eyes of some demonic hound, as I might have expected on Dartmoor – they were the eyes of an otter.

'Otter!' I cried involuntarily. I was still recording, and listening to it now I can confirm that I was so taken aback that I forgot to include the indefinite article.

The time it took me to utter the word was about equal to the time it took the creature to spin round to its right and dive back into the water. In a flash it was under the bridge. I ran across to the other side to catch a glimpse of it swimming away but it was far too canny for that. Hard though I pinned my ears back I never heard another sound. It had disappeared as completely as a deer in a wood.

It did not matter that our encounter had lasted but a second or two, for I had seen an otter, the first I have ever seen in the wild outside Scotland. Indeed, I had not merely seen an otter but an otter and I had looked into each other's eyes. Sadly, I suspect the otter saw little of mine for I must have dazzled it right royally with my bicycle light. I suspect otters do not live for such moments anyway. Once safely back at its holt, I imagine the conversation with its partner went something like:

'Have a good hunt, dear?'

'Nah. Bumped into another of those blasted bipeds – you know, the tall ones that smell of crisps.'

'What a bore.'

'Yes. Funny thing with this one is that I think it was on fire.'

Otters used to be a common sight in the rivers of Nottinghamshire. However, these largely nocturnal creatures were given pest status in English law in 1566, by which time a dog, the otter hound, had already been especially bred to hunt them. Come the 17th century, wealthy Nottinghamshire landowners, perceiving the otter as a threat to their estates' well stocked fish ponds and the game fish in their rivers, began paying out large sums to anyone who killed them. The persecution continued until quite recent times. In the 1950s certain landowners in the county were still inviting the Buckinghamshire Otter Hounds onto their estates for some 'sport'. The few otters that survived past this time succumbed to the pesticides that leached into the waterways.

Happily, a great deal of money has since been spent cleaning up the River Trent and, as a result, otters have been making something of a comeback in the county. The fact that this one had made it so far from the Trent – some 15 miles distant – is no small cause for celebration.

Buoyed by this unexpected meeting, I rode away telling myself that I no longer cared about the approaching storms. Furthermore, in the time that I had leant my bike against the wall of the bridge, a spider had spun a web across my handlebars. I was clearly becoming at one with Nature and, like King Lear, would face whatever cataracts, hurricanoes and oak-cleaving thunderbolts were thrown at me with the stoic pragmatism that all Nature's creatures adopt, at least all those used to British weather.

I cycled away from Birklands, keen to get to Welbeck Park while it was still dry. I made my way along a track through woods that led to a wider track through denser woods in the midst of which I passed a parked car. Two men who may or may not have been up to any good sat in it, talking in low voices. When I was at last obliged to take to the road, there was not a single vehicle troubling it. Had it not been for the bicycle I was riding I could well have believed that I had been conveyed back to a time when transport meant a horse.

All was tranquil. The road was pitch black and as silent as thought. My world had been contracted to the narrow corridor that my bicycle light cut through the heavy air. Perhaps it was just the effect of the darkness and the humidity but I seemed to be cycling inordinately slowly, as if the atmosphere had turned to porridge or an unseen hand was pulling on my brakes. Before long, I was pulling them on myself, for out of the corner of my eye I caught sight of the outline of some kind of monument. I had nearly reached it when I jumped out of my skin. A bird as large as a buzzard – which indeed might well have been a buzzard – appeared without warning in the air space just a couple of feet above my head. I say 'appeared' but in reality I heard the startled whipping of feathers on air and felt on my face the sudden gust produced by its wings, but I did not see it.

I had evidently disturbed the bird from its perch, which, on closer inspection, turned out to be something called the Bentinck Fountain. It had clearly seen glories greater than the poor laurels tossed its way now. Once it had been cherished as an effecting feature of a grand estate. Now it stood apologetically by the side of the road, its empty trough sticking out like a beggar's imploring hand. A plinth held a large bas-relief plaque so eaten away by the elements that in a few years' time it will be impossible to make out that the fountain was built to honour one Lord George Bentinck. The one-time Conservative member of parliament for King's Lynn and co-agitator with Disraeli in opposing the repeal of the calamitous Corn Laws 'died suddenly near this spot on the 21st September 1848 in his 47th year'.

The pathos of this attempt to exaggerate his lifespan beyond his 46 years was matched by the infelicity of the stray Remembrance Day poppy someone had secured to the plaque.

The neglected monument was now but a resting place for probable buzzards. A frog clambered clumsily about its base, no more interested in the subject of the memorial than I had been as a schoolboy suffering that special torture that is the study of the Corn Laws. Yet on this night this dried-up fountain had at least taken on the status of a place, for me at any rate. After so many trees and so much apparent nothingness between the trees, I felt a strange pleasure from being *somewhere*. If someone had asked me for my location right then I could have confidently declared, 'I'm at the Bentinck Fountain.' When I cycled off again it felt like I was striding out from the shade of a solitary outcrop back into the enveloping desert.

This sense of being subsumed into a wilderness, far from dissipating when I reached the village of Norton, was rather greatly amplified. Not a single person stalked its tidy streets, nor was there any a car to disarrange the silence. The houses, lovely old houses that had seen things they would never tell, showed not a single light – no ghost of an ARP warden would feel compelled to rise from the grave tonight. I could not even detect the manic flicker of a television behind a curtain. The only indications of life came from the fidgeting clouds of midges and the snoring of some large unseen animal sleeping out in a field just beyond the nosy jurisdiction of the streetlights. A sign proclaimed that the penalty for dropping litter was a chastening £1,000, though this presupposed that there might ever be anyone here to drop it. If I had been a Hood-like outlaw on the run this night, I would have been more than satisfied with the dearth of potential snoopers ready to report my whereabouts to the authorities.

It was as I entered Welbeck Park, just after the witching hour, that the first flashes of lightning rent the sky. I counted the seconds to the thunder in the time-honoured fashion, but the thunder never came. I wondered if perhaps I might get lucky and the storm might pass me by altogether. Under a sky lit up at ever shorter intervals, the track and I zigzagged towards an entrance to Welbeck Abbey, an elegant ducal residence.

At one point my map showed the path crossing a field while running right alongside a long row of dashes regularly interspersed with tiny squares and marked with the thrilling legend *Tunnel Skylights*. Unfortunately, my attention was distracted by my attempts to register whether the droplets of water I began to feel on my face and hands came from the sky or were blown my way from the various sprinklers doing duty in the field. By the time I reached the wood at its far end, the distinction was academic. The first crashes of thunder coincided with the opening of the heavens.

Taking shelter beneath the pines I weighed up my options. The map showed the Robin Hood Way cutting a swathe through mile after mile of woodland. Although this was clearly welcome – aside from keeping some of the rain off, it also meant that I had at last reached another significant part of Sherwood Forest – I was keenly aware of the fact that being beneath trees in a thunderstorm is not without its hazards, the chief one of them being the possibility of being struck by lightning. I dithered. The rain began to come down in such torrents that even the mature conifers surrounding me could not keep me in the dry state to which I had become accustomed. Meanwhile, the sheet lightning of the early minutes of the storm had become rather dramatically forked. Eventually I cracked and made a decision – I would return to the nearest place of refuge I had passed on my way here. Bracing myself, I headed out into a frankly diluvial outpouring. Unhappily, I chose what looked like a better path than the one I had arrived on but it soon became very muddy. Unwilling to return to the woods and start again, I ploughed on but became disorientated, heading this way and that before I found my way. I was therefore somewhat damp by the time I hauled myself and my bike off the road to stand with my back pressed into the deepest recess of a bus shelter.

At Night

The Germans have a word – *Sturmgeheulunbehagen* – which means 'the discomfort brought on by howling storms'. Had you asked me at the time, I would have admitted to feeling more than a modicum of *Sturmgeheulunbehagen* as I pedalled furiously back and forth through the rain while lightning tore up the sky in great jolts of unthinkable power and thunder battered my eardrums.

However, there is a flip side to the word, and that is the pleasure that comes from being spared the discomfort brought on by howling storms – a sort of *Sturmgeheulunbehagenverschonungserleichterung*, if you will. It's something I think a lot of us experience: even the simple act of remaining snug and dry while a brief shower of rain beats against your windows can bring pleasure.

It was, then, with no little sense of contentment that I unpacked a few bits and pieces from my pannier – a smoothie of Polish origin I had purchased in a corner shop, some nuts and raisins, and my radio – and sat down on the floor to witness the storm taking out its fury on my new world. This latter consisted of an impassive stretch of tarmac, a fence, a single streetlight bright enough to read by even though it was on the far side of the road, and a couple of signs advertising the busy business empire that Welbeck Park has become.

I took in my temporary lodgings. The shelter was made of wood that came right down to the ground, so there were no chilling draughts whipping around my ankles. Its roof was not leaky and it was deep enough to ensure that the floor was dry. The one drawback was that there was no seating of any kind, so I took out a handy little mat for sitting on that I habitually carry about with me for just such occasions and settled myself down. This was not exactly what I had envisaged when I had imagined how my night in Sherwood Forest might go, but it would provide me with a decent enough home until the storm abated. Although there can be fewer more public homes than a three-sided bus shelter on an A road, the night and the elements had rendered it as private as if it had been a house in a gated community. Even when, every five minutes or so, a car swished by, I could rest assured that its unseen driver sped by oblivious to my presence, tucked away in the corner as I was. Robin Hood, in all of his wanderings, could not have wished for a safer haven than this.

I put the radio to my ear and listened for a few minutes to the BBC's World Service, that friend of many a lonely voyager of the night. Something or other to do with business was happening in Nigeria. The familiar pattern of chatter back and forth between London and Lagos – or perhaps the correspondent was in Abuja: to be honest I wasn't paying all that much attention – seemed at once both otherworldly and domestic.

The storm soon moved on to fresh hunting grounds further north, leaving the stage to the steady thrum of the downpour. The streetlight exposed the presence of intermittent gusts that pushed the rain one way and then another. Occasionally, a frog would appear in the road as if it too had come down from the clouds and I would feel compelled to leave my little corner and rescue it. By the third one I had become quite competent at catching them and from then on spent no more than about ten seconds in the rain each time I carried out the procedure.

For the rest of my stay in the bus shelter I stared happily out into the rain, not really thinking about very much at all. A blanket of sleepiness slipped itself around my shoulders and I enjoyed the slowness of mind that it brought on.

Had I been the 5th Duke of Portland, the rain, no matter how hard it fell, would not have proved an issue. Those *Tunnel Skylights* I had missed in the field helped illumine just one section of miles of tunnels that the peer had had built beneath his estate. Somewhat unjustly known as the 'Mad Duke', William John Cavendish-Bentinck-Scott inherited his title in 1854 at the age of 53 and over the next 18 years created one of the more astonishing underground complexes Britain has to offer — a warren only those skylights now keep from dwelling in perpetual night.

The tunnels were voluminous enough to allow a wagonette pulled by four horses to pass along them. Of the more extensive undertakings, one led half a mile or so from the stables to an icehouse near the Greendale Oak, a tree his great-great-grandfather had eviscerated by cutting a massive arch into it and driving a coach-and-horses through to win a bet. Another took the duke a mile and a quarter towards Worksop station where his wagonette could be driven straight onto a special flat wagon which was then coupled to a London-bound express.

The tunnels were by no means the end of the duke's ambition. He also ordered the digging of a five-room library and, most ambitiously of all, a subterranean ballroom which still exists today and, when completed, boasted the largest indoor floorspace uninterrupted by columns in the whole of Europe.

Inevitably, rumours spread that the tunnels were used by the duke to fulfil romantic assignations, much in the style of the Prince Regent and the underground passageway from his Royal Pavilion at Brighton to the house of his mistress Mrs Fitzherbert (a myth as it happens: the tunnel led to his stables). The truth is somewhat more edifying. Poverty in the area was widespread and persistent during Victoria's reign. The excavations the duke had carried out were designed to provide jobs for labourers and craftsmen, an estimated 1,500 of whom were employed on the venture.

At Night

I drifted happily in and out of visions of wagonettes charging up and down the tunnels but rarely did the rain show any signs of abating. If I'm completely honest I confess I was slightly disappointed on those occasions when it did ease slightly because I didn't then feel that I was extracting the full benefit of being under cover.

After an hour and a half, for no other reason than to instil some variety into my life, I left and cycled headlong down the road to another bus shelter I had noticed earlier. Garlanded with ivy, guarded by nettles and provided with fetching wooden arches, one of which served as a grand entrance, my new abode constituted a leap of several rungs up the property ladder. Furthermore, it contained a bench that ran the whole length of the back of the structure. This was luxury indeed.

I stretched out on my back, listening to the rain and was overwhelmed by a feeling of utter contentment. I was alone in a place I did not know in rotten weather at gone three in the morning but I would not have been anywhere else for all the gold in the Sheriff of Nottingham's treasury. As a firm believer in John Stuart Mill's dictum, 'Ask yourself whether you are happy and you cease to be so,' I did not try to trace the possible source of this quiet rapture but simply revelled in it. I have been afflicted too many times by that curiously bleak despair that the small hours of the night can impart not to welcome its more munificent twin with open arms.

My joy was made complete when a song thrush in a tree across the road announced its existence to the world. Lovely though the woodlark's *lu-la lu-la* undoubtedly is, how could anyone choose such minimalist stylings over the veritable symphony of tunes served up by its passerine cousin?

At length, the drumming of the rain slowed and then halted altogether. The downpour had lasted more than four hours. I rose from the bench rather stiffly and headed back up the road to resume my journey. The conifer wood, when I reached it, was still dripping from the deluge.

The path through it became a hollow way, a narrow lane sunk 10ft or more into soft red sandstone. As I walked along it – the ground being too uneven to cycle in the dark – my bike light picked out what appeared to be ancient hieroglyphs. On closer inspection they were somewhat less intriguing: merely endless sets of initials etched into the rock over the decades and, by the worn and weathered look of them, over the centuries too. However, at least some minor mystery had been instilled by means of the gnomic message 'GAIT CON' which someone had felt important enough to incise here in large letters.

Comic relief of sorts was provided by a birch – not a species of tree always known for its playfulness. This one, though, had seen fit to grow on the very edge of the precipice. It had then leaned in so that it appeared to be keeling over into the hollow way. What it did not want you to see was the cheeky finger it had projected over the edge of the little cliff right down to the ground to keep itself balanced. Had I been on the run this night, one good swipe of an axe would have sent the tree toppling into the path of my pursuers. Robin Hood is the sort of man who one feels would always have had a little axe swinging from his belt for just such an exigency. To my shame, I had not even brought my Swiss army knife. I had much to learn.

The going became easier once the path had climbed back up to ground level and I was pleasantly surprised at what little effect the rain had had on the dirt beneath my wheels. I breezed through woods filled with silver birches, their trunks shining in whatever light came their way. It was not the Sherwood Forest of the imagination – that crown clearly belonged to the oak wood of Birklands – but it was heartening that such expansive tranches of woodland still existed, even if they were but remnants of the ancient royal hunting forest.

Eventually I reached a road and a sign announcing that I had come upon Clumber Park. The Robin Hood Way skirts it for a while before picking its moment to plunge in at a spot where, though the track was wide, the underwood consisted of bracken that reached over my head. A little parcel of great willowherb had staked out a tiny corner while a smaller patch of rosebay willowherb was hanging on grimly in another. A couple of dock plants made up the remainder of this laudable but almost certainly vain resistance.

It was only when it struck me that I had been able to delineate between the two sorts of willowherb without the aid of my bike light that I realised it was no longer too dark to see. I had been so deep in the forest when day had broken that the event had been lost to me. It was, at any rate, not one of those dawns over which the poets swoon. The sky was so dank with leftover clouds that there had been no sunrise as such. The day had sloped in with a hangover and did not wish it to be known that it had clocked on for duty.

I pressed on into the woods and it became night again. In one particularly gloomy spot, a fancy metal signpost warned me, somewhat unnecessarily, that I was 786 miles from Inverness and 504 miles from Dover. Perhaps this was intended to scotch any harebrained notion I might conceive to cycle to either for breakfast.

When I emerged from the trees I found myself at the official entrance to Clumber Park. The 3,800-acre estate, for centuries the property of the Dukes of Newcastle, is now owned by the National Trust. Though shorn of its stately home, which fell into disrepair and was demolished just before the last war, the grounds still sport a walled kitchen garden, Europe's longest double avenue of lime trees (as records go, I suspect this is one that will raise the pulse of only the hardcore dendrologist), a secondhand bookshop, a café, the inevitable gift shop and a gothic chapel. The rest is parkland, woods and an ocean among lakes so thick with pondweed that it seemed a continuation of the lawn.

After the unruly forest this all appeared very mannered and out of keeping with the night I had spent, for even the bus shelters had retained a certain rustic simplicity. There were geese aplenty, grazing the well-kept lawns bordering the lake, but not a soul disturbed this scene of faded ducal eminence, blurred into wonderful watercolour by the dim light and my tired eyes.

I dismounted and wandered through the grounds in a bit of a daze, stopping for a lingering look towards the tea room which would remain cruelly closed for many hours to come. I tried to distract myself from thoughts of tea and buns by inspecting a dismantled miniature gun battery which was added by the 5th Duke of Newcastle in order to 'threaten his one-third scale model frigate'.

I scurried through Hardwick Village, a collection of Victorian cottages that had been built for labourers in an elegant neo-Elizabethan style and must have seemed a wonderland to impoverished workers back in the late 1800s. After a few hundred yards of the

A614, I turned southwestwards to luxuriate in a further 3 miles of uninterrupted woodland.

I found myself on a narrow cycle path carpeted with red gravel. On both sides I was hemmed in by high impenetrable hedges, or what appeared to be hedges but was in fact merely extraordinarily dense woodland. Dawn's feeble light was all but snuffed out and I felt myself once again being hauled back into night. I kept expecting gaps to appear or for side paths to join the trail but I looked in vain. Although the tops of the trees rarely met to form a canopy over my head, I did get the distinct impression that these woods suffered me to pass through them. It would only take one summer of neglect and the path would disappear completely, red gravel and all.

Shortly before the Lambert Simnel rebellion was crushed by Henry VII at the battle of Stoke Field, roughly 15 miles to the south of Clumber, there had been a few days of skirmishing in Sherwood Forest. In this jungle, where there was hardly room to thrust a pikestaff, let alone swing a sword, it struck me how difficult it would be to kill someone in a wood with a piece of metal or even with a bow and arrow (a fact which, incidentally, must have comforted any outlaws sheltering here). Clearly, the exchanges must have taken place in more spacious oak woods but, even there, once off the path movement becomes complicated. Far better to be slaughtered out on the open fields, as the Yorkist soldiers duly were.

At Night

Even these tightly packed trees couldn't keep the day at bay forever and the tunnel through them began to be suffused with a ghostly light. My night in the forest was over. I had not seen badgers but I had locked eyes with an otter. I had spent more time than I had bargained for in shelters made of trees rather than under trees themselves, but even there I had encountered frogs and a song thrush and a quality of contentment that, I suspect, only the night knows. I had become acquainted with slumbering woods of oak, with seemingly limitless stands of silver birch sleeping to attention with one eye open, and with woods so dense and tangled they dozed leaning one on top of another like battle-weary soldiers.

Furthermore, the reputation of woods as places that become sinister and forbidding after dark had not been borne out at Sherwood, whose trees had not contorted themselves into ghastly shapes to form unholy silhouettes against the moon. There had been no menace in the dark heart of the forest – only nightjars and foxes and glow-worms. Had it not been for the storm and my fear of attracting the attentions of a bolt of lightning, I'm confident I'd have even discovered some dry niche large enough to protect me from the rude world and its downpours.

Pondering such pleasantries, I had not long passed through the far side of the wood and was back on the outskirts of Birklands and journey's end when disaster struck: a puncture. For some reason that is obscure to me even today, I had neither repair kit nor spare inner tube with me. I was 5 miles from the nearest railway station and it had begun to drizzle. I cried out in anguished torment, secure in the knowledge that only the trees would hear.

Then a miracle occurred. The first human being I had seen since the two suspicious men in their car in the woods all those hours before came riding up the path towards me. With a look of concern that betrayed the fact that he had heard my sorrowful bleat, he pulled up and asked if he could help. Then, as if pulling an arrow from his quiver, from the bag on his back he withdrew not only a spare inner tube but a spare inner tube that was precisely the size I needed. Rejecting all offers of payment, he stayed with me and chatted while I made the necessary repairs and cycled away only when he had assured himself that my bike was ready for the road again.

My benefactor's name was Lee and he professed to come from Meden Vale, a former mining village just along the road from our encounter. It is to him that I dedicate this chapter, for while Robin Hood may or may not have existed, it is heartening to know that there is still someone roaming the forest and doing good deeds. Who knows, in a few hundred years' time the nation may celebrate the legend of a mysterious man who was said to appear in the forest whenever anyone got into difficulties, no matter what time of day it was. His name is Lee of Sherwood.

4

Mountain

Spend the night alone on the summit of Cadair Idris and you'll wake up either a poet or a madman.

Who could possibly resist such a dare? If you win, you come down the mountain a poet. If you lose, you probably won't remember what it was like to be sane anyway. I booked my rail ticket to west Wales almost immediately.

The Cadair Idris challenge is said to have its origins in the practice of Welsh bards who sought inspiration by climbing the mountain and spending a night close to the stars. This would also go some way to explaining the non-inclusive language in which it is couched. I imagine that today there's no prohibition on women attempting the feat, though it would seem a harsh blow indeed for a woman to return to society not only shorn of her senses but also changed into a man.

It's by no means the only example in Britain of a gauntlet laid down to the brave or the foolish to spend a night alone somewhere that boasts an unwholesome reputation. Indeed, there are some instances in which the challenge is reversed and someone brave or foolish vows to spend a night alone somewhere undesirable in order to unmask a well-established superstition as hokum. It has to be said that the latter examples almost always end badly, but then there isn't much of a story if the person undergoing the ordeal is proved right.

Whichever way round the stage is set, there is almost always an old and forbidding building involved in which some sort of alleged paranormal activity takes place. A typical example is that of 50 Berkeley Square in London. Now the address of an apparently peaceful antiquarian booksellers, in the 19th century it became known as London's most haunted house. As is the case with the Wisht Hounds out on Dartmoor, the belief took hold that anyone who saw these ghosts – one of which was said to be a shapeless black mass that was hideous to behold – came to an untimely and unpleasant end. A certain member of the nobility poured scorn on such notions and duly offered to spend the night in the most haunted room. His bravado lasted but a few hours. Shortly after midnight, he got the fright of his life and promptly lost the power of speech. Shocked beyond all telling, he was unable to communicate what he had seen in the room and died soon afterwards.

What makes the Cadair Idris challenge so interesting is that it has neither a spooky old house nor some obvious supernatural presence to face down. We are not even given a hint as to what might cause the transformation of the lone sleeper. There's just a mountain top and the night.

Some sources like to give the dare extra spice by adding a third possible outcome: that the person who sleeps a night on the summit will never wake again. In very cold weather, of course, there's every chance of that cheery forecast becoming reality since you're nearly 3,000ft up and exposed to the elements. In July, however, armed with a tent and a sleeping bag, I felt my prospects of waking again were at least evens. Furthermore, although I had bought my rail ticket some time in advance, I had skilfully managed to pick a relatively warm and dry night for my attempt.

I can heartily recommend the cycle path along the southern shore of the Mawddach Estuary. It ushered me from Morfa Mawddach, a tiny railway request stop near the mouth of the river, all the way to the hamlet of Abergwynant, entertaining me along the way with wading birds and posses of cyclists calling out jovial greetings in the evening sunshine as they passed me bound for holiday cottages in Fairbourne and Barmouth. An exacting climb on back roads took me to the car park at Tŷ Nant and the beginning of the Pony Path, the longest but gentlest of the three routes up Cadair Idris, rising 2,000ft over about 3 miles.

I was keen to witness the sunset from the highest of the mountain's three peaks, Penygadair. Accordingly, I set off at 7pm although the sun was already low enough by then that it hurt to look west, so fiercely was it cannoning off the sea some 5 miles away. The air was unnaturally still, as if someone had finally found that pesky butterfly in the Amazon, informed it of the wider ramifications of its actions and persuaded it to stop flapping its wings.

The Pony Path takes its name from the pack animals that carried flour, butter and other essentials around the mountain from the little village of Llanfihangel-y-Pennant to the market at Dolgellau, and that were later employed to lug Georgian thrill-seekers up to the Penygadair summit. The route comprises three quite distinct stages. There's an initial steep section that takes walkers southwest. This is a bit of a tease because the summit lies to the southeast. However, once onto a ridge, the path heads straight for its destination and the going becomes easier until, at the very last, the incline becomes more precipitous as it pushes up to the top. On the way I met two lone walkers and, near the summit, a pair of mountain bikers. They were all heading downhill, which was fine by me because if I was to take the challenge in earnest I must have the summit to myself. I confess I had not thought through a plan of action had I found myself joined there by others with the same intentions as me beyond bursting into inconsolable floods of tears.

Given the sheer number of legends that swirl around southern Snowdonia's highest peak – including one that claims that it was King Arthur's seat of power - it's surprising that none have encroached on the poet-or-madman myth. There are, for instance, no phantom dogs to terrify or dismay the pilgrim, even though the mountain forms part of the hunting ground of Gwyn ap Nudd, ruler of the Celtic otherworld Annwn. The howling of Gwyn's red-eared dogs was said to be a harbinger of death to anyone who heard it. Worse still, the victim then suffered the misfortune of having their soul herded into Annwn by the pack. One could be forgiven for thinking that the people of west Wales and the people of Dartmoor had been comparing notes, for Gwyn's dogs do sound an awful lot like the Wisht Hounds.

The name of the mountain means 'Chair of Idris' and relates to a giant who seems to have been responsible for the seemingly random locations of a great many of the huge boulders that lie on and below the mountain, having developed a fondness for throwing them. His legend may have been based on a man called Idris ap Gwyddno ('Idris son of Gwyddno'), a 7th-century prince of Meirionnydd, who was also known as Idris Gawr ('Idris the Giant'). Welsh history enthusiasts will not have to be reminded that one of the nation's great heroes, the poet Taliesin, was discovered as a child floating in a basket in the waters of a river crossing land belonging to Idris' father, Gwyddno. It wasn't just any old basket either, but the famed Hamper of Gwyddno Garanhir, which is now celebrated as one of the Thirteen Treasures of the Island of Britain.

However, there is no suggestion that Idris stalks the dreams of sleepers on his mountain top, hurling boulders at them to turn them mad with fright. Neither does Taliesin appear at the stroke of midnight to dish out metrical and lyrical skills, despite the fact that he is revered as one of the greatest of Welsh bards and would thus be a perfect fit for the story. You will also search in vain for any mention of magic hampers being distributed among the favoured. It must be said that that is particularly regrettable because any food a person put in one was increased a hundredfold, which would set them up as a wedding caterer for life.

There's a sense in which this very absence of information is the myth's strength. Each of us is left to imagine what on earth it is that happens up there between dusk and dawn that could cause someone to become mentally ill or magically endow them with a deftness in the handling of quatrains and eye rhymes.

When I arrived at the summit, Penygadair ('head of the chair'), I was greeted by four ewes and two lambs.

Perhaps greeted is an exaggeration, for none of them paid the slightest attention to me. Rather, one of the lambs declared herself unhappy with life, standing all alone and bleating for all she was worth. Having made her feelings known, she trotted back to her mother, who might perhaps agree with her if she hadn't long since resigned herself to her fate. They began to eat side by side and the tantrum was forgotten. I was glad of their company, for I would not see another living thing close at hand until the morning when a pair of swallows came scything through the sky and a young and adventurous herring gull attempted to coerce me into sharing my breakfast.

The climb from Tŷ Nant is really not all that taxing and had taken only 80 minutes so there was no flopping down exhausted by the trig point that marks the summit. However, it is still the highest peak in southern Snowdonia. The view from the top might have been specially designed to bring the poet out of the most prosaic of visitors, especially when there is the added attraction of a ravishing sunset.

Directly below lay Llyn y Gadair, a lake so obviously created by glacial action that I'm surprised it hasn't been filled in with the ashes of generations of besotted geography teachers. From my eyrie I could see several other classical features of a cirque glacier – the huge boulders or 'erratics' strewn untidily around (more probably by the action of ice rather than Idris Gawr); the huge bowl carved out by thousands of years of ice flows, creating the illusion of a giant's chair; and the rocky outcrops known as *roches moutonnées*. These last are not, as is often supposed by those keen to show off their classroom French, 'sheep-like rocks'. The term was coined in 1786 by mountaineer Horace-Bénédict de Saussure who fancied he saw in them a resemblance to the wigs then à la mode among the French upper classes. The hairpieces were slathered in mutton fat, hence '*moutonné*'.

To the west, beyond the seaside resort of Barmouth, the sun still blazed off the sea but now more kindly, as if to warm rather than blind. I peered for some time in that direction at what I imagined to be clouds before I realised that they must be the low mountains of the Llŷn Peninsula caught in haze on the far side of Cardigan Bay. I did a slow lingering 360-degree sweep of the countryside around and below me, filling my eyes with mountains and ridges, glaciated valleys and minuscule settlements, and marvelled at how this jumble of crumpled topography fitted together so pleasingly. It was as if Constable had painted a landscape based on a drawing by Picasso.

There's a stone shelter at Penygadair but I'm more of a tiny tent man, so I pitched camp and cooked myself some dinner. The battered aluminium pot on the stove reflected the slowly darkening moods of the sun. When the meal was ready, I pulled on a fleece, sat down and waited for the night to come upon me.

At this point, I should confess that there was a time long ago when I yearned to be a poet and even had illusions that I had some talent in that direction. For several years I stalked the land performing my work under the name – ill-advised now I look back on it – of Stonking Ralph Kierkegaard. At the time I said I was influenced by the Scottish poet, songwriter and wit Ivor Cutler but the reality is that I aped him shamelessly. Hoping for the great man's blessing on my nascent career, I sent him a booklet – necessarily self-published – of about 40 of my poems. Weeks passed and then, much to my surprise, I received a letter written in a quivery hand, old beyond its years. The envelope also contained a dozen or so little stickers Ivor had had printed in white and gold which bore such messages as 'befriend a bacterium' and 'THE ESSENCE OF A LABEL IS TO INFORM, BUT——NOT THIS ONE, AMIGO'. He had returned the booklet with a box drawn around the three lines within it that he had enjoyed. Needless to say, they were the three lines that most cravenly mimicked both his style and content. I had imagined a childhood of habitual soakings while out walking with my mother and siblings along the High Street:

If it was acid rain
We would lift our faces to the sky

And feel the fizz of the water on our tongues

There used to be a line in between the 'sky' and the 'And' but Ivor felt it would be better 'scrubbed' and I trust his judgement on such matters.

I think I knew from that moment on that I would have to earn a crust some other way. In all honesty it didn't really matter what that other way might be for I assumed quite reasonably that by the time the bold and thrusting 21st century came along I'd have to settle for being an astronaut like everyone else.

When I came across the Cadair Idris myth, with its promise of curious happenings at 2,928ft, it felt like I was being given a gift. I don't know if there is any correlation between altitude and endorphin release but I feel happy just being on mountain tops, or even just up on high, open ground. On this score I'm as one with the French-Algerian philosopher-cum-goalkeeper Albert Camus. He couldn't understand why anyone would want to explore underground, confining themselves to dark constricted spaces, when they could climb hills and mountains and enjoy fresh air, big skies and freedom of movement. I was therefore not altogether unhappy that the challenge to spend a night in Chislehurst Caves in Kent was not an option open to me. It had been brought to an abrupt end in 1985 after a very strange incident indeed that bears retelling for it has become one of the classic night-time challenges gone wrong.

The Chislehurst Caves are not actually caves *per se* but a chalk mine that has created an extensive maze of tunnels and caverns. They were used as an arsenal in World War I, an air raid shelter during the next global conflict, and are now a popular tourist attraction. If the many reports of paranormal activities are to be believed, the caves are home to a host of ghosts in both human and animal form, innumerable unexplained noises, spectral orbs and poltergeists.

The so-called Haunted Pool had a particularly disturbing reputation – so much so that a small reward was established in 1950 for anyone who managed to spend a night there alone.

The pool's reputation dates back to the story of a flint knapper who, sometime in the 1700s, is said to have murdered his wife, weighed her body down with chalk and dumped her in the water. The White Lady, as the unfortunate woman's ghost is known, is purported to appear at the poolside, crying quietly. The atmosphere at the pool is often described as unnaturally cold or unsettling, though it's feasible that a draught of cold air and the power of suggestion might fuel such fancies.

The rules for the challenge were duly laid down. The participant could take in nothing but a sleeping bag and six candles, and must stay by the pool all night. The guide who escorted him or her in would give a promise to return in the morning and would leave a trail so that the contestant could find their way out if necessary.

At Night

The gauntlet was taken up on many occasions. Some faint-hearts apparently lasted just a few seconds and ran out after the guide almost as soon as they had been abandoned there. Others left the pool area and, disorientated, found it impossible to follow the trail back out of the caves. They took refuge elsewhere in the chalky labyrinth, wishing the hours away until the guide came to call for them in the morning.

One man is said to have lit all his candles at once. As they were about to burn out he realised his folly and grabbed one and hurried away with it. This caused the candle to blow out, as one might expect, but in his terror the man hurtled on in the inky darkness, running straight into a low part of the ceiling and knocking himself out. He was still out cold when discovered by the guide the next morning but he was refused the reward on the grounds that being unconscious somehow violated the spirit of the challenge. This seems particularly harsh since the fact that you can take a sleeping bag in does rather suggest that being unconscious is tacitly permitted.

Surprisingly, perhaps, official cave guides were themselves allowed to take the challenge should they wish. Most were clearly too canny to do so but in 1985 two guides – Dave Duker and Chris Perry – decided to take up the cudgels. With a commendable sense of the theatrical, the date they chose for their attempt was Hallowe'en. Little were they to know what notoriety their bid would achieve.

Some might say that the two men crossed the line from the theatrical into the hubristic by carving a plaque into the wall near the pool the day beforehand to commemorate what they imagined would be a successful 12-hour vigil. They had also managed to circumvent the rule stating that the challenge must be taken alone by promising to spend the night in different locations around the Haunted Pool. A tape recorder was placed between them to ensure that they did not communicate with each other (one assumes this was a reel-to-reel affair recording at a very slow speed). The men took the precaution of locking the entrance to the caves behind them once they were alone to ensure that their friends – who were spending the night just outside the caves as a support team in case anything untoward should happen – could not sneak in and play tricks on them. The two guides tossed a coin to see which positions they would take up around the pool. Chris won and moved to the spot where they had carved their plaque.

All went well until about 2.30am, when Dave was woken up by the sound of Chris screaming. The recording of what happened next reportedly suffers from a lot of background hiss but Chislehurst Caves expert Brian Williamson has made a transcript of the words and noises that could be identified.

From this we know that Dave runs over to Chris, who is still in his sleeping bag, and makes increasingly desperate attempts to get him to respond. Chris merely moans. Dave decides to go and get help but realises after he has gone that Chris has the keys to the door. He returns and asks Chris to give him the keys. Chris is still in no state to deal with enquiries. Dave eventually finds the keys in Chris' pocket and leaves to rouse their friends. While Dave is gone, the tape picks up the sound of Chris uttering further moans and there are some noises consistent with him rolling about in his sleeping bag.

The rescue party enters. One of the group points out that Chris looks in a 'bad state'. He is certainly still uncommunicative. He is asked repeatedly if he is all right but answers with his by now customary groans. As the rescuers discuss what to do next, Chris can apparently be heard shouting out, his cries echoing away around the darkened caves.

'We were doing quite well,' Dave opines, 'then *that* happened.'

Since he was unable to walk, his friends carried Chris out of the caves and took him to hospital. He was given a thorough check-up but the only thing obviously wrong with him was some bruising to his shoulder. An X-ray revealed a severe dislocation. He subsequently underwent an operation that left him with a 6-inch scar. The medical opinion was that his arm had been yanked upwards with considerable force, perhaps in a bid to drag him along the ground. However, when Dave had initially run over to Chris he had noticed that his friend's arms were both inside his sleeping bag, making this hypothesis somewhat unlikely. Chris himself has no recollection of what occurred.

The incident caused the challenge to be cancelled and no one has been allowed to attempt it since, although a film crew for a ghost-hunting television series did stay overnight in 2008 and emerged with enough footage to air two hour-long programmes. Remarkably, the ill-fated Chris continued guiding visitors around the caves until 2004. Dave, meanwhile, found the football pools more lucrative than the Haunted Pool. He won them just a few weeks after the night in the caves and gave up guiding for good.

The events of Hallowe'en 1985 tend to overshadow the fact that, in the 35 years in which it was on offer, the reward was actually won once, by a police officer named Tony Bayfield. However, his night was far from tranquil. He reported that after a while in the semi-darkness by the pool he had a sense that he wasn't alone. Edging away from the water his foot struck a piece of flint on the floor. He picked it up and had an idea. In order to focus his mind on something other than whatever might be lurking in the darkness nearby, he spent the rest of the night carving a crude drawing of a horse into the cave wall. It was this spot that Chris Perry later chose when he won the coin toss, on the grounds that if one man had successfully spent the night there, it was a safe enough place to be.

At Night

The crudely incised horse can still be seen today, right next to the plaque etched by Perry and Duker.

Bayfield wasn't able to explain why he chose a horse as his subject. Brian Williamson has speculated that he may have been influenced in some supernatural psychic way by a disaster that occurred around 1860 when part of the roof of the cave by the pool collapsed, bringing the stables above down with it. The ghostly screams of terrified horses have been reported in the vicinity.

I hardly expected my own night, way up on the summit of Cadair Idris, to be quite so filled with incident. Indeed, I was rather ashamed at feeling so happy to be there. While I freely admit to experiencing the occasional pang of loneliness on my night-time excursions, nothing approaching that visited me on the mountain. It made me optimistic about the outcome of the affair – the gods, or whoever was responsible for the nocturnal metamorphosis, would have to work pretty hard to send me from my current state of mind to insanity. Perhaps if I had had no means of shelter and had been obliged to spend the night huddled behind some rocks with an icy wind chilling my bones and rivulets of rainwater trickling down my neck, I might have been set on my journey towards psychosis. On the other hand, such an experience might just as well have been the spur towards some great lyrical endeavour. After all, the Reverend Augustus Toplady is said to have found inspiration for one of the English language's best-known hymns, *Rock of Ages,* after sheltering from a storm in a gorge in the Mendips.

I was also distracted from introspection by the sheer beauty laid out before me. It doesn't usually work for me like that. Out of necessity I do a lot of travelling on my own and there's been many a bittersweet moment when I have been confronted by some thrilling landscape or prepossessing object and have yearned to be able to share it with someone. Smartphones and social media make that possible at one remove, of course, but it's a route that has never tempted me and, in any case, someone proclaiming to like your photograph is a very poor cousin to being with someone who is experiencing what you are experiencing and whose eye you can meet when you both break into a smile.

In the failing light to the west there was Fairbourne and Barmouth, connected by the sinuous curve of the long railway bridge that spans the Mawddach Estuary almost at its mouth. On the other side of Cardigan Bay, the small town of Pwllheli had lit itself up. I was lord and master of the valley of the Afon Deri – the puny headlights of cars making their escape up it from Machynlleth could be squashed by any one of my all-powerful fingers. The tumble of hills and mountains that had captivated me on my arrival at the summit now turned from green to grey, as if the slate inside them were bleeding out. The only jarring note came from a couple of antennae I had not noticed earlier. These revealed themselves by their columns of warning lights, all of which were red, as if they were vying with each other in a never-ending contest to be the region's least friendly traffic lights.

Over the sea some half-dozen clouds, now given a dirty orange veneer by the dissipated sunset, stood motionless like a row of parked airships. 'That's as far as we're going today,' their pilots had declared. 'We'll start again in the morning.' I watched as they all slowly dissolved into the night, charcoal smudges on a sepia canvas.

As they did so, the first stars took the stage. Vega and her early rising friends sashayed on to announce that the night was about to commence. When it did eventually begin in earnest, which was not much before midnight, I noticed something extraordinary. If I looked up I could see constellations in the sky: if I looked down I could see constellations on the ground.

Above me, the firmament was a riot of diamonds – Ursa Major, Cassiopeia, Pegasus, Andromeda, Gemini, Pisces, Hydra, Leo, along with other constellations whose identification I have never quite got to grips with even after hours of staring at maps of the night sky. Below me, terra firma sparkled with its own luminaries – Caerdeon, Bontddu, Pen-y-Bryn, Dolgellau, Corris Uchaf, among other constellations I could not identify for certain even after hours of staring at maps of southern Gwynedd. Meanwhile, every 15 seconds, the plucky little lighthouse on St Tudwal's Island West winked at me like a satellite. The only spectacle the Earth could not replicate was the Milky Way, that ghost of the welkin. It stretched itself across the sky, an indeterminate presence, a whisper.

That was the other element that my surroundings had in common with the sky above them: the quiet. It was astonishingly quiet in fact. The sheep had settled down and were quite possibly already asleep; the few cars I could see made their way dumbly along the valley floor; the inhabitants of Caerdeon, Bontddu et al had retreated behind their curtains; not an insect was left on the wing. The only indication that I hadn't been struck deaf was the gentle flick and flack of the sides of my tent on those rare occasions when the air stirred itself into movement.

Time itself seemed to tiptoe around for fear of disturbing me. Midnight at last crept away to be replaced by the opening hours of a new day. A chill in the air I had long been expecting, given the exceptionally clear sky, passed its fingers over the back of my neck and I shivered. Looking around I became aware again of the stone shelter and I decided to see what sort of home it would have made had I been stranded here without a tent.

Instead of a door there was a long porch with a stone bench built into the wall at the end. I would sit here later, as the night grew colder, because it still afforded a sumptuous view across the Mawddach Estuary to the starlit mountains beyond. From the bench there was a 90-degree turn into the shelter, a design that obviated the need for a door here either. Inside, blank walls made with large rough stones hewn from the mountain itself were relieved by a few very small windows set near the low ceiling. These faced the summit rather than the view, not that anything could be seen from them anyway. The brutal concrete frames in which the glass was set and the metal grills outside them gave the place the rather unfortunate feel of a prison cell, while the uneven floor of large stones spoke more of a castle dungeon.

The corrugated iron roof was held up by mighty wooden beams – whose porterage here must have caused a headache or two – and held down outside by hefty stones and a rudimentary system of wires and rods and bolts. It was the only evidence I had that the wind sometimes paid a call here. Home comforts consisted of a long narrow bench running around the walls and a block in the middle of the floor that served as a table. The claggy smell that makes its home in stone hovels was present but not at all pronounced. On the table there were the remains of a fire far too small to have burnt away the damp, so perhaps what wind does make it along the porch and into the shelter ventilates the innards sufficiently to keep them dry.

Outside, my torch found evidence of a possible second room, but whether it fell down or was never built I couldn't tell. The shelter is so large – a school class caught out by a summer storm could fit in here at a pinch – that I can't imagine there would be much call for an annex, even given the mountain's popularity among walkers.

In all, the shelter represents a fantastic achievement by the people who built and maintain it. Over the years it must have been a welcome sight to countless folk surprised by a turn in the weather or simply ill clad for altitude. The rustic use of the mountain's own stone and some thoughtful positioning ensure that it doesn't detract from the beauty of the scene. I was glad that I was not spending the night inside it though. I know that fans of the bivouac pour scorn on us tent dwellers for cutting ourselves off from nature, and I myself have slept out under the stars without protection on many occasions, but I still feel sufficiently at one with my surroundings with a thin layer of ripstop nylon between them and me. The sail of my fly-sheet picks up every nuance of the wind and amplifies every drop of rain into a drumbeat. The smell of the grass and cowpats and dew insinuate themselves into the inner sanctum. There is also something comforting about being inside a tent and listening to the goings-on outside even if, as I've confessed, I cannot always identify them: the scuff and haw of the wind, the complicated patterns of the rain, the scurrying of rabbits, the hooting of owls, the croaking of rooks, the rustlings of hedgehogs and the susurrus of who knows what creature going about its nightly business. Also, there's very little chance of being woken by a sheep having an investigative nibble at your hair.

As far as I could tell, the powers that be had not yet gone about their work of transformation so I decided to give them a chance while I was unconscious. I duly turned in at about 2.30am. I had expected the stars below me to have faded by then but they were still burning as strongly as the myriad stars above. I slept as soon as my head hit the pillow, a restful, dreamless sleep that lasted until well past the dawn.

The next morning, on my return to what passes for civilisation, the bright warm sunshine drew the sweat out of me even though I hadn't an inch to climb. The scenery lay stretched out below me in glorious waves of green and green and green and green. I checked myself. Was my insistence on giving every shade of green beneath me the same monicker proof that I had awoken a poet of immense stature who required but few words to conjure images in his readers' minds? Or was it evidence that I'd actually just completely lost it? Secretly, I suppose, I was hoping to end up both poet *and* madman, like Blake.

To test which I had become, I decided to spend the walk down the mountain penning a poem about my experiences on Idris Gawr's stronghold.

· *★* · ·

Cadair Idris
Not so much a test of fitness
More a sort of lofty witness
To my mental state
Fastness of giant rocksmith
Home to Gwynedd's half-man-half-myth
Once a Prince of Meirionnydd
Now master of *my* fate

Mayhap he'll make of me a poet
Rhyming 'word' with 'sword' as though it
Really does but doesn't know it
Until *I* emerge
Sonnets steaming from my keyboard
Eschewing words like 'coast' for 'seaboard'
As a v bored Second Sea Lord
Might harpoon a dirge

Keats and Yeats and Burns all worthless
Wilde and Nash and Lear all mirthless
William Wordsworth? Rendered Wordless
When I'm a poeteer
Metaphors like honey bees
Mellifluous as similes
With no little victual of litotes
To drip into your ear

· ⋆★ · ·

Or perhaps he'll send me mad…

Deranged

Demented

Barmy

RAGING

Unhinged

MaNiC

Frenzied

Raving

Hysterical

Unstable

CRaZEd

Delirious

CONFUSED AND

DAZED

OFF MY MIND

AND OFF MY TROLLEY
Marbles missing
Gosh and golly
Like the hero of *Where's*
Wally
WHAT'S HIS NAME NOW?
CAN'T REMEMBER
Brain's all frazzled
GOt distemper
of the mind
And of my reason
My à la mode is so last season

See where this ecstatic erratic lies
The Blurred Man of Alcatraz arise
HOWLING like Ginsberg
Contemplating jazzercise
I'm scared of my shadow
I'm scared of Dubonnet

At Night

THE RED-EYED HOUNDS
AND THE ROCHES MOUTONNÉES
I am the March Hare but I'm UP on all fours
My lift isn't stopping at any of the floors
I've bats in the belfry and hens in my chick flick
I'm a whole magic hamper short of a picnic
Psychotic, disturbed, I get nothing quite right
I RAGE, RAGE against the drying of a knight
I'M MAD, I'M SAD AND I'M STRANGEROUS TO KNOW
I do need a weatherman to know which way
the winds blow

But reader dear
I ask you to ponder
Upon a worse fate
Awaiting up yonder
Than becoming a poet
Or a man with brains ascatter...

If I know that I'm the former
But folk think that I'm the latter

I shall let others reach their own conclusions as to
which side the coin had fallen that night I spent alone
on Cadair Idris.

5

Sky

It was Dante, apparently, who claimed to cherish the view of the sky above all others. Like most people, I expect, I only came by this nugget through exposure to E M Forster's *A Room with a View*. Sadly, I have never felt a sufficiently pressing desire for self-improvement to plough through the great Italian poet's *Divina Commedia* so am not in a position to say whether he preferred a dome of the purest azure or a night-time firmament bristling with twinkling lights. They each have their attractions, of course, but I like to think that the man who gave the injunction 'Follow your own star' was a night sky kind of guy. After all, a wash of perfect blue may have a soothing quality to it, but for those yearning for a taste of the infinite, there is nothing like gazing upon a void riveted with innumerable sparkling diamonds.

In Britain we seldom tire of commenting upon the divide between urban dwellers and those who live in the countryside but one difference not usually noted is the two camps' experience of the night sky. While country folk are generally used to seeing panoplies of stars whenever there's a relatively cloudless night, the light pollution generated by towns and cities typically prevents those living in its glare from discerning any but the brightest of heavenly bodies. However, even in the deepest countryside the night sky is often obscured by artificial lighting, whether it be from the street lamps lining the main thoroughfare of a village or the security floodlights illuminating a farmer's barn. Thus, the only way to guarantee a view of the stars, planets, comets and satellites in all their natural glory is to head for one of Britain's Dark Sky Parks.

And so it came to pass that I found myself striking out west from Dumfries in southwest Scotland on a late summer's eve. My destination was the Galloway Forest Park, home to Britain's first ever Dark Sky Park, a designation bestowed upon it in 2009. In order to win this accolade from the International Dark-Sky Association, stringent measures had to be put in place to ensure that light pollution is kept to an absolute minimum every single night of the year. England has its own Dark Sky Park in Northumberland, while the Exmoor and Brecon Beacons national parks are now apparently dark enough to merit a slightly lower-tier status. However, I had heard such excellent reports of Galloway Forest Park that I was determined to spend a night there. A little research revealed that a reservoir on its southeastern edge known as Clatteringshaws Loch came particularly recommended since it overlooked the park's heart of darkness. At 8pm, with the sky still a diaphanous blue, I freewheeled down a hill and turned onto a drive leading to the loch's visitor centre.

Although, of course, it's difficult to predict with complete assurance that a certain place will turn octopus black at the coming of night, I had been encouraged that, in the 7 miles I had cycled from the little crossroads village of New Galloway, I hadn't encountered a single car. This at least suggested I was bound for wilderness of some sort. The terrain had also proved promising – evolving from dense forest on one side of the road to dense forest on both sides. The only artificial light I had seen had come from a digger deep in the midst of a thicket which was engaged in knocking down some trees.

The people of Dumfries and Galloway are notoriously thirsty types, a reputation borne out by the fact that the Clatteringshaws reservoir was exceptionally low. The visitor centre had long since closed for the night so after a quick pilgrimage to the nearby Bruce's Stone – marking the spot where King Robert is said to have taken a breather after defeating the English in battle – I cycled around the loch in search of a secluded place to camp.

It's apposite that the first park in Britain to be devoted to the observation of the night sky should be in Scotland since it was a Scot, Thomas Henderson, who was the first person to measure the distance to a star.

As it turned out, his calculation that Alpha Centauri was 3.25 light years away was a little undercooked (it's currently believed to be a little over 4 light years distant) but in the 1830s even having an intelligent stab at the mind-bending distances involved was something at which to marvel. Unfortunately, due to a lack of confidence in his own results, Henderson delayed publishing them until 1839, by which time one Friedrich Wilhelm Bessel had made his own calculations public with regard to a star named 61 Cygni and so scooped the glory.

I'm a bit of an obsessive when it comes to finding the best possible place to camp when out in the wilds and was pleased to find a flat spot tucked in the lee of a rock a little way up from the loch shore. By now it had grown dark enough to make out Alpha Centauri in the southern sky. Our nearest star is actually a group of three stars. One pair orbits slowly around their common centre of mass, like two dancers locked in a never-ending waltz, while a third, a red dwarf called Proxima Centauri, sits in front of them. If you're a stickler for detail, it's this last star that is actually the closest to Earth. Taken as a single unit, though, Alpha Centauri forms the third brightest star in the sky. It provides a useful service in that, once you spot it, you know you've latched onto Centaurus, its near namesake constellation which, as its name suggests, bears a passing resemblance to a centaur. Ancient peoples were keen on seeing mythical human–equine hybrids where the rest of us might only perceive random patterns of stars. Look across a little way to the east in summer and you'll come across the constellation of Sagittarius, which is also named after a centaur, though to modern British eyes its brighter stars unerringly form the outline of a teapot.

Perhaps because I'd been too wrapped up in finding Bruce's Stone I hadn't immediately noticed Vega, always one of the first stars to show itself in the northern hemisphere. It's relatively close and twice as large as our sun, so is an easy one to identify, especially in the warmer months of the year when, in conjunction with the brilliant Deneb and Altair, it forms the Summer Triangle. In the old days – and I do mean the old days here because we're going back 14,000 years and beyond –Vega was the northern pole star. Just like Mae West's joke about Snow White, she drifted, and was supplanted in the hearts of navigators by Polaris. Redemption is at hand, though, for in another 11,000 years or so Vega will reclaim her title and whatever intelligent beings are around then will look to her for a northward bearing.

For now, however, she must content herself with holding the distinction of being the first star aside from the sun to be photographed by humans. On the night of 16 July 1850, two astronomers from the Harvard College Observatory captured her likeness using the daguerreotype process, crudely exposing a sheet of copper that had been plated with a fine coat of silver. For all the pioneering efforts of the Harvard scientists, it's true to say that Vega looks rather better in the flesh. I even had high hopes that, as night drew on, I might see her wearing the silken scarf of the Milky Way across her throat.

While waiting for the final vestiges of twilight to give themselves over to the night, I cooked some dinner over a little stove. When I looked up again, the first signs that I might not have chosen the ideal date for a night of stargazing began to reveal themselves. Wispy clouds, only a touch lighter than the sky behind them, had advanced from the southeast to form small patches of nothingness where stars should have been.

At least Sirius, the dog star, was still there. Although outshone by Venus and, very often, Jupiter too, Sirius is the brightest star seen from Earth. This is slightly misleading because it actually consists of two stars very close together: Sirius A and its small white dwarf companion Sirius B. It was another Scot, Williamina Fleming, who was one of the first astronomers to identify white dwarfs. This remarkable woman's story is all the more extraordinary because she made her discovery at a time when women were forbidden even to look through telescopes at the night sky in case they swooned at the romance of the stars.

Hailing from Dundee, as had Thomas Henderson before her, Fleming was born in 1857 and emigrated to Boston, Massachusetts with her husband at the age of

21. Abandoned by him a year later despite the fact that she was pregnant, she went into service as a maid for Professor Edward Charles Pickering, who happened to be the director of the Harvard Observatory.

Given the status of women as *personae non gratae* when it came to observatories, it came as no surprise that the team Pickering employed to pore over photographic plates in search of new stars was exclusively made up of men. However, he became so dissatisfied with their efforts that one day he sacked them en masse. According to legend, he declared that his Scottish maid could do a better job. Whether or not he said this, the assertion was correct. Williamina Fleming was found to have a genius for astronomy and was soon devising a whole new way of classifying stars according to the amount of hydrogen that could be observed in their spectra.

She was placed in charge of an all-female team known as the 'Harvard Computers' who were given the onerous task of sifting through hundreds of thousands of photographs of the night sky. In nine years Fleming personally catalogued over 10,000 stars. She also discovered 310 variable stars (bodies whose light fluctuates), 59 gaseous nebulae – including the famous Horsehead Nebula – and 10 novae (massive nuclear explosions on white dwarfs). In 1910, she published her findings on white dwarfs and sealed her reputation. It's as well she did because she caught pneumonia the following year and died.

Just in case you feel that this has nothing to do with you and your life, you should know that our own sun is destined to become a white dwarf once it runs out of hydrogen, though admittedly that shouldn't be for a year or two.

While Sirius was still beaming brightly, I had lost bits of the Big Dipper, every lay sky-watcher's favourite star formation. There are three very good reasons behind the popularity of this seven-star supergroup. Firstly, you can call it pretty much what you want: along with the Big Dipper, both the Plough and even the Saucepan are acceptable. Secondly, it is one of the few arrangements of stars that actually obviously looks like something – and that something is indisputably a saucepan with a bent handle. Thirdly, as every schoolchild used to know, you can use it to find Polaris, the North Star, and thus orientate yourself, no matter what sort of pickle you've managed to get yourself into. All you need to do is draw a line up from the two stars that form the edge of the saucepan furthest from the handle. Carry on until your imaginary line is about five times longer than the distance between the two saucepan stars and you'll hit Polaris, shining out in an otherwise empty patch of sky.

This is by no means the only way of pinpointing the North Star. For example, you can pop an imaginary lid on top of the 'W' formation of Cassiopeia, take a line up at 90 degrees from the left-hand end of it and, once that line is double the length of your lid, there's Polaris. Alternatively, if you can count and have eyesight that can gauge degrees of luminosity with astonishing precision, you'll be able to identify Polaris on the grounds that it's the 48th brightest star in the sky. However, in the absence of Cassiopeia or superhuman abilities, the Saucepan remains a reliable signpost. Furthermore, because this little group of stars is circumpolar – i.e. it revolves around the pole star – it never sets, which means you'll see it at any time of night if the sky is clear.

The only disappointing thing about the Big Dipper/Plough/Saucepan is that it is not actually a constellation but rather what is known as an asterism: a group of stars that forms a recognisable shape. It constitutes a section of Ursa Major, the Great Bear – roughly speaking its haunch and tail.

Returning from a heavenly saucepan to attend to my earthly one, I finished cooking and ate my dinner disconsolately under the slowly disappearing stars. As Rabbie Burns himself pointed out, 'The best laid schemes o' mice an' men/Gang aft a-gley.' Mine were ganging very a-gley indeed. What's more, although the countryside around was as exceptionally dark as one might hope for in a Dark Sky Park, I could still see two lights around the loch. One, further north, was vague and perhaps came from a torch used by another wild camper. The other, however, was a fixed light on the shore straight across the loch from me that blazed away over the water as if hoping to catch an escaped prisoner swimming across it. Did it denote the presence of an angler? I couldn't think of who else might want to employ such a powerful light. I wanted to shout out across the loch to the miscreant to inform him that he was violating a local by-law but the night seemed too quiet and still to sully it with coarse hollering. Also, I managed to fool myself that my voice would not be heard two-thirds of a mile away. This was ridiculous, of course, given that sound is carried better both at night and also over a large body of water. I chose instead to grumble quietly to myself.

To take my mind off it, I concentrated on seeing all that I could see between the clouds. I was pleased to catch a glimpse of the Milky Way threading itself across the heavens. Galileo was the first to pin a definitive explanation on this enigma which had puzzled the ancients. He put his eye to his telescope and discovered that it was simply made out of stars. Four hundred years later no one is quite sure just how many stars, but it's likely to be between 100 and 400 billion.

Vega had disappeared, turning the Summer Triangle into a Summer Line. Cassiopeia had gone too, as had most of the Plough. I sat at the entrance to my tent with only the sound of distant sheep for company, telling myself that, if I was patient, the clouds would eventually disperse. The unnaturally stagnant air around me told a different story but, I reasoned, if the clouds were moving to mask the stars, they might continue to move and reveal them again.

Unpredictable weather is one of the more equivocal pleasures of British life. You can create an area as dark as the Mariana Trench but if the sky itself won't play along, you might as well stare up at the heavens with a blindfold on. It is no good even attempting to explain to the gods of weather that you have a book to write, for their response is a silence as profound as that of the stars themselves. The only thing to do in the circumstances is assume a stoical air and consider that the very best characters are forged in adversity.

The moon was on the wane and tonight was hitting its last quarter, that cusp where it's a toss-up as to whether it's waning gibbous or waning crescent. Any argument over its state would have been entirely academic, however, for it too had vanished without trace. Soon there was not a single star to be seen either. Such was the efficiency of the clouds in knitting themselves together into a vast ventless quilt – a sure sign of the dastardly stratocumulus variation – that I felt as if I would never set eyes on another star again.

I wouldn't have minded so much had the clouds brought rain with them, or even the threat of it, but these were purely killjoy clouds with no other aim than to spoil my view. All I could do as I sat looking out at the faint outline of the hill on the far side of the loch was admire the work of those who oversee the light emissions in the Galloway Forest Park. There is no getting away from the fact that, stray anglers aside, they have made it very *very* dark indeed.

I consoled myself with the thought that, since I was staying in the nearby village of Moniaive for a few days, I could simply cycle back on one of the nights and enjoy the stars then. In the meantime I decided to go for a little blunder around the loch, and found myself toppling over onto the grass almost before I'd started.

I had read on an old plaque nearby that Mary, Queen of Scots had passed this way on 13 August 1563 though the notice was silent on whether she too had lost her footing stumbling about these parts in the dark. Moonless nights here in the mid-16th century would have been just as Stygian and Mary often found herself forced to travel in circumstances that precluded the showing of a light. Furthermore, she was prodigiously tall for her times – just an inch off 6ft – so her high centre of gravity would have facilitated such tumbles. However, it occurred to me as I brushed myself down and then did some sums on my fingers that when she came by she was yet to turn 21 and, despite already being a widow, had accumulated few of the black marks against her name that would ineluctably lead to her execution. And so my romantic vision – in which a fugitive queen and I, though separated by three and a half centuries, had been drawn together by a mutual want of physical coordination – died a death.

However, it did make me wonder whether that most peripatetic of sometime monarchs was so famous that her every movement was worthy of note or if Clatteringshaws Loch had been so sidelined by history that its biographers grasped at any brush it might have had with celebrity, no matter how fleeting. The news, also carried by the plaque, that it might not have been Robert the Bruce who won a battle near here but his lesser renowned brother Edward suggested that the latter might be true.

Unwilling to besmirch the darkness by turning on a torch and unable, even with my pupils stretched to the size of marbles, to make out anything but the most conspicuous of deviations beneath my feet, I decided to curtail my prospective promenade along the shores of the loch. Instead I sat on a rock, enjoying the tranquillity of my circumstances and pretending not to mind that I was in one of the darkest places in Britain and yet could not see a single solitary star.

The loch had succumbed to the wiles of the treacle night and was so soundly asleep its waters did not even deign to lap against the exposed mudflats. Only my rhythmical breathing disturbed the stillness of the void. I closed my eyes and then opened them again and enjoyed the fact that it made so little difference. However, even the acute nirvana-esque exhilaration gained from perching on a rock and staring into nothingness can begin to pall after a while, and since it had become apparent that the vast bank of cloud above my head was going nowhere, I called it a night and sank into sleep where I lay.

. ⋅ ★ ⋅ .

When I opened my eyes again, I looked out upon a profound mystery. The blank canvas I had gazed up at before I drifted off into the arms of Morpheus had gone. In its place, someone had installed a chart of thousands of stars − not just the constellations but myriad unfamiliar stars too. These fainter dots of light freckled the constellations to such a degree that they looked even less like the wild beasts and mythical figures they were supposed to resemble. Stretched out across this confusion of tiny lanterns was the Milky Way, a sort of aurora borealis as seen on a black-and-white television.

The transformation from darkness to light was so complete that it did make me wonder whether I wasn't still asleep and dreaming it all up. Even my friend on the other side of the water had packed up his industrial-strength floodlight and had gone, leaving the reservoir in almost pitch darkness. Here at last was the night sky as it was meant to be seen.

Depending on whose figures you believe, there are between 5,000 and 8,000 stars that can be seen with the naked eye, of which roughly 2,500 can be viewed from any one place on Earth. Only those with no romance in their soul would attempt to count them,

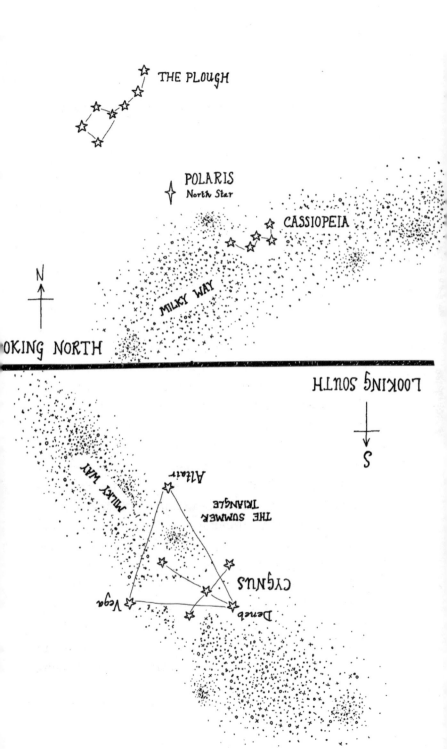

THE PLOUGH

POLARIS
North Star

CASSIOPEIA

MILKY WAY

N

LOOKING NORTH

LOOKING SOUTH

S

MILKY WAY

Altair

THE SUMMER TRIANGLE

CYGNUS

Vega

Deneb

so I was happy to let myself be overawed by the scene as a single immense artwork instead. Obviously, even at this great distance from the stars it was not possible to take the whole lot of them in at once so I allowed my gaze to roam around, enjoying each little patch of pulsing silver specks in turn.

Of course, the sky is not filled only with stars (and satellites and numerous bits of space junk) – planets too sweep in and out of our firmament as their orbits bring them close to our own. When this occurs, Mercury, Venus, Mars, Jupiter and Saturn can all be seen without the need for a telescope. Of these, Mars and Venus are the most readily identifiable. Mars, the so-called Red Planet, is just that. Its colour is caused by iron oxide, a fact I've always found pleasingly parochial, for it is the very same element that I have seen turn little streams and rivulets red in English woods and Scottish glens.

Unlike our own planet, however, Mars enjoys a somewhat eccentric orbit around the sun. Its oppositions – when it is closest to Earth and on the opposite side of our planet to the sun – occur roughly every couple of years, but every 15 or 17 years its perihelic oppositions bring it particularly close to us.

It was one such pass in 1877 that allowed Italian astronomer Giovanni Schiaparelli to produce the first detailed map of the planet. He famously marked certain features on his map 'canali', which can mean both 'canals' and 'grooves' in Italian. English translators almost always used the former term, however, which led to the widespread belief that there was water on Mars. If there was water then it stood to reason that the planet must also be able to sustain life. Thus the Earthling's obsession with the idea of there being life on Mars was born. This played itself out in innumerable sci-fi stories, comic strips, films and a song by David Bowie. Such was the belief in the possibility of an invasion of Earth that Orson Welles' infamous 1938 radio adaptation of H G Wells' *War of the Worlds* – in which the future film-maker had hostile Martian spaceships land in New Jersey – sent many Americans into a panic when they mistook it for an actual news broadcast. It took the Mariner and Viking spacecraft missions to show that the chances of there being any life at all on Mars were remote indeed – and so the curtain came down on what had been a bestselling show.

Venus, meanwhile, makes up for its lack of a dramatic red hue and improbable inhabitants with its extraordinary brightness. It is second only to our moon in its brilliance and can even cast shadows, so if you ever see what looks like an astronomically dazzling star in the sky it'll be our sister planet. Since it's the second rock from the sun, and thus takes less time to orbit our star than we do, it laps us every 584 days. Before this occurs it is visible just after sunset and is known as the Evening Star – a name beloved of poets and doubtless bemoaned by astronomers.

After it overtakes us on our race around the sun, it is magically transformed into the Morning Star and we must begin to look out for it just before sunrise.

Lying by the waterside, it was neither Mars nor Venus that I scanned the skies for but our solar system's most memorable planet, Saturn. I peered in vain for a glimpse but it seemed to have disappeared from the sky. On Skomer, a couple of months beforehand, I had seen it as a very faint dot of light lurking quite low in the southwest. Even back then I'd missed by some way the best time to see it, which had been on 10 May, its opposition date. It was bright and easy to spot around that time because it appeared to rise in the east as the sun set in the west. Saturn's opposition occurs every 378 days on average, so if you move the date on by a little less than a fortnight each year and search for it then you'll get it about right.

Peering at it through a telescope from the little Welsh isle, the planet still made for pretty spectacular viewing nonetheless. I knew, of course, what Saturn and its rings looked like – no one who has ever spent more than, say, a week in school could possibly be ignorant of it – but I was ill-prepared for what I saw. If it were not an unfortunate turn of phrase in the circumstances, I would say that I was star-struck. It was my first ever telescopic meeting with this great celebrity of our solar system, and it looked *exactly* like it does in the pictures. I laughed involuntarily, as I fear I might if I ever happened to meet one of my

Earthly heroes for the first time. It was the best part of a billion miles away but I felt as though I could pick it up in my hand, pop it in my pocket, and perhaps tie a bit of string around it in the morning and use it as a yo-yo.

My view of the rings was of their upper (northern) side and it was only afterwards that I wondered when I would be able to see them from below. I consulted some erudite sources and it turned out that if only I had taken the trouble to seek out Saturn between 11 February 1996 and 4 September 2009 I could have feasted my eyes on the underside of the rings. It will be almost a decade until any of us can do that again. This is all because the planet is rather sluggish when it comes to orbiting the sun, taking almost 30 years over it. For nearly half of this time it presents us with one side of its rings. There follows a period where we look straight at the very edge of the rings before they finally tip up or down sufficiently for us to view the other side. The astonishing thing about the rings themselves, aside from the fact that they are composed of almost nothing but humble water ice, is that, though they are roughly 155,000 miles wide, they're astonishingly thin. Estimates of local thickness range from 1,000 yards to a piffling 30ft – less than the length of a London bus – which is why they virtually disappear when you see them edge on. As is so often the case with the universe, the more you look into it, the odder it shows itself to be.

At Night

I confess that my inability to spot Saturn in the mesmerisingly congested sky above Clatteringshaws was not something that caused me even a moment's anguish. It was enough to be lying here, a tiny supine form beneath an infinity of stars. The stupendous gulf between them and me was so above and beyond what my mind could comprehend that whenever I tried to think about it, I could feel the neurons in my brain go into meltdown, like a crashing computer. Even working it out in some sort of scale that I could understand did not help: for instance, if I travelled towards the very nearest star I could see at a not unsprightly 1,000mph, it meant I would still take... the best part of three million years to reach it. The very *nearest* star! Far better not to think at all.

Instead I let myself fall into a pleasantly disorientated reverie. I found that if I kept my eyes fixed on the sky for long enough, I lost any sense of distance or proportion. Should I stretch my hand out I might well be able to pluck one of those stars down after all, just as I had once hoped to capture Saturn. When I closed my eyes it felt like the ground beneath me was lifting me gently up to meet the beckoning cosmos. Only a hint of a zephyr playing upon my cheek reminded me that even if I were effectively turning my back on Mother Earth, she wasn't going to let me go quite yet.

I realise that it might appear from the previous paragraph that I had come across some interesting mushrooms while putting up my tent that night.

However, I defy anyone to be exposed to such a spectacle and not feel even a little overwhelmed by it or find their sense of perspective altered.

Caught up in the everyday business of life, it's all too easy to believe in our own importance. We fight our respective corners; we jostle for position; by often inappreciable increments we attempt to improve our lot. Some of us even saddle ourselves with the thankless task of correcting other people's grammar. But gazing up into what is, after all, merely a tiny fragment of the universe, it brought it home to me once again just how very insignificant we are. We cling on to a speck of dust drifting about in one of countless galaxies. Do our sorrows and triumphs, our living and dying, really mean all that much in the grand scheme of things? Staring up into the abyss, I found it difficult to believe that they did.

I knew that, inevitably, all the minutiae of my life would become important to me again tomorrow – when the sun rose above the eastern horizon, putting an end to the magic show and drawing the blinds on the universe once more. Tonight, though, I was content to exchange all that for a comforting sense of kinship with the twinkling lights above me. For we are all ultimately made of star dust and we will all doubtless return to that state again one day.

PART TWO
TRAVEL

6

Train

Visitors to Fort William may be forgiven for thinking that the eponymous stronghold no longer exists. Even when I went and stood right in the middle of it, on a patch of recently mown grass sandwiched between Loch Linnhe and the railway station, I didn't get any sense that I was inside a fortress that once held a garrison of 1,200 English soldiers and successfully withstood a full-blooded attack during the Second Jacobite Rebellion. If anything, given the landscaped banks and the long, brightly painted planters placed at the top of them, one might mistake this for a bijou park.

The fort was not, as might be supposed, torn down by Scots enraged at the Sassenach colonisation this building symbolised. For a clue to the source of this act of cultural vandalism, we need look no further than the railway station across the road. In 1889 the North British Railway Company seized the fort by compulsory purchase from one Christina Cameron Campbell, a local laird who had done much to preserve it. The company knocked down the greater part of the fortress, running railway lines right through it to service a station built at the southern end of the town. The fact that in 1975 the station was blithely relocated to the town's northern end, and all the tracks through the fort pulled up, makes the wanton destruction all the more mystifying. To lose a historical landmark and gain nothing more exciting than a small grassy open space seems like a poor deal to me.

Having read this rather dismal tale on some information boards – which also dispensed the unhappy news that the massacre at Glencoe was planned within these walls – I dropped down to the shore of Loch Linnhe. From here at least some of the fort's walls became visible, even if they only reached from the beach to ground level. I looked at my watch – it would soon be time to board the train. I just had time to get a quick peek at Ben Nevis before I left.

Fort William is a popular starting point for those wishing to climb Britain's highest mountain. It's possible to walk straight out of town, along Glen Nevis, and then head on up. Dusk was coming on but there was still plenty of light in the sky and I knew the peak was only a few miles away, roughly to the southeast. Wherever I looked, though, there was no mountain remotely big enough to be Ben Nevis. It was only much later that I found out that it hides itself away behind a ridge. There are apparently one or two places in Fort William from which you can see the ben, but I had clearly not been standing in them.

Having not really seen a fort and then not having seen Britain's highest mountain at all, it was a mood of mild disappointment with the world that hung over me as I traipsed across the busy road to board my train. I noted darkly as I passed through the characterless station that if there was one building in Fort William that no one would mind being flattened it would be this dispiriting affair, apparently designed – if that is not too flattering a term – by someone of the opinion that the planet was not nearly dull enough.

Yet all this was forgotten the moment I walked onto the platform. No one who has any sense of adventure in them whatsoever can clap eyes upon a sleeper train and not feel their heart quicken. I would be stepping on board here in the Highlands, right next to if not quite within eyeshot of the highest point in the land, and I would not be getting off until I had reached the confines of the largest city in Europe. Breathing in the crisp Highland air, clean to my urban lungs even when fouled by the traffic cruising the Fort William bypass, London seemed a place impossibly far off. Yet here I was, boarding this hotel on wheels that had been laid on to take me there. Don't tell me there's nothing of the fairy tale in that.

. ⋆ . .

Sleeper trains between Scotland and London have a longer pedigree than you might imagine. Monet was painting *Sunrise* and Tolstoy was penning the opening chapters of *Anna Karenina* when the North British Railway Company unveiled overnight services connecting Glasgow Queen Street and Edinburgh Waverley with London King's Cross.

Since these so-called Lowland trains were established in 1873 they have been joined by three Highland services that convey night riders between the English capital and far-flung Aberdeen, Inverness and Fort William – the five routes going by the rather fine collective name *Caledonian Sleeper*.

The train that heads north to Fort William has even acquired its own nickname, *The Deerstalker*, since it enables those taking it to be up and about and harassing large wild ungulates from an early hour. I made various enquiries but was disappointed to learn that the southbound train from Fort William has yet to be christened. I thus spent perhaps too much of the journey down attempting to come up with an appropriate soubriquet. The obvious choice, if the hat theme were to be pursued, would be *The Bowler*, after the headgear every man in London is known to don before setting off for work. Or there was *The Howler*, after Victorian novelist Arthur Morrison's description of the capital as a 'howling sea of human wreckage', but that seemed a shade too glass–half–empty. In the end I settled on *The Vortex*, on the grounds that the capital has, for centuries, been a whirlpool that has sucked in prodigious quantities of people and resources and, on occasion, spat them out again. Also, the phrase 'I'm travelling down on *The Vortex* tonight' has a pleasingly sci-fi ring to it.

It should be added that the *Caledonian Sleeper* is famous, at least among rail enthusiasts, for being the longest train in service in Britain. On the southern stretches of its routes these leviathans of the network run to 16 coaches. They only relinquish this title on Saturday nights when, due to apparent lack of demand and the need to allow staff at least some of the weekend off, there is no sleeper service.

· ✦ · ·

I stood on the platform and scanned its length for someone who might know where I should put my bicycle. I don't have many rules by which I live my life but I've notched up two when it comes to sleeper trains. In Britain, you get the same cabin whether you have a first or a standard class ticket. Travelling first class does, however, secure you exclusive rights to the cabin (and a fun bag of toiletries) whereas with a standard class ticket you are more than likely to find yourself sharing the cabin with another passenger of the same sex. As a travel writer I'm sometimes in the enviable position of receiving complimentary first class tickets – I would feel guilty about this but such occasions brighten an otherwise penurious life. When this is the case I ask in advance – all the while attempting to assume a cool and insouciant mien – what is the earliest possible time I can board. I then turn up a minute after this time – the 60 seconds appended in order not to appear too keen – so that I can enjoy the maximum amount of time on the train. It does not even matter if I have brought nothing to read for there is a surfeit of signs in the cabin, some of which are reproduced in the following pages for your delight and delectation. Their content ranges from what to do in an emergency (a veritable essay covering all possible eventualities) to how to tell if the fire alarm is going off (this also comes in French and German so gives passengers the chance to brush up on both). Thus I have more than enough to engage my interest until it's time to depart.

If I'm sharing with strangers, the process is reversed – I'll leap on at the last moment so that I have to make as little small talk as possible. I'm sure other people who use sleeper trains are fascinating creatures deserving of rigorous study but I find there's something crushingly awkward about being in such a confined and intimate space with someone I don't know from Adam and having to attempt to keep up some sort of conversation with them.

In this case, it was as well that the railway company had not asked me to share or I might not have known my cabin mate from Eve. The attendant,

Eddie Redmayne, or at least a young man very similar in appearance to the Oscar-winning British actor, had me down on his list as a woman, presumably on account of my name. This is an error that happens with some frequency so I am accustomed to forewarning whichever authorities I happen to be dealing with that I am not, in fact, female. However, where my sex is of no importance I've found it's often worth keeping shtum just to witness the look of confusion passing across the face of whoever it is I'm seeing for the first time. Redmayne, to give him his due, recovered better than most, joking that I might conceivably board the train a man but arrive at Euston a woman. This is quite brave since it is only the second sentence he has ever spoken to me. I counter that I have packed a wardrobe capable of dealing with all eventualities. It's noticeable that from that moment on he calls me 'sir' at every opportunity. I cannot quite make out if there is a little glint in his eye each time he does so.

I stowed my bicycle. Redmayne had broken the bad news that I should have to get off the train at Edinburgh Waverley and move my rusting steed to the portion joining us from Aberdeen.

'One passenger had a £2,000 bike on board and it got damaged,' he explained apologetically, 'so ever since we've had to ask bike owners to get out and move their bikes themselves.'

At Night

It was also news to me that we should be hacking drunkenly across country to Edinburgh rather than keeping to the west as was the route implied by the Highland Sleeper timetable. (It was only later that the mystery was resolved: the detour to Edinburgh is kept secret in order to stop people from attempting to end their journey there, such is the irresistible allure of Auld Reekie.) Ordinarily, the business with the bike would have been a slight irritant because this train pulls in to the Scottish capital around one in the morning. However, since I was not intending to sleep at any point anyway, I had no objections to stretching my legs at Waverley.

'If you'd been on the train coming up you'd have had to have got out at four!' Redmayne added in attempted consolation.

I grimaced. That is a state of affairs that must be deeply annoying to those who might understandably assume on boarding that they would be awoken only when the train arrived at, say, Inverness at a somewhat less harrowing hour of the morning. To have to get up at 4am, dress, leave the train, shift a bicycle, board, undress and then attempt sleep again is not part of the dream.

All too soon the train jerked into life with a jolt and then pulled smoothly away. The already arduous route south to London is immediately sabotaged by Ben Nevis and the imposing cluster of mountains over which it reigns, forcing the railway line northeast

170

in search of a corridor to wriggle along. The familiar restful rhythm of the wheels started up – the *di-dum-di-DUM di-dum-di-DUM* pattern that old trains favour. This being a carriage built in the early 1980s, another noise accompanied it: the sound of a thousand angry mice squealing their disapproval at the decision to get going. To be fair, it should be said that it is unlikely that the intricate layers of screeching *are* generated by a thousand angry mice. However, it did sound as if every piece of metal that made up the carriage was scraping against every other piece of metal. Personally, I quite enjoyed this atonal overture – this slice of rolling Stockhausen if you will – for it took me back to many another sleeper journey I'd made across Britain: not just up to Scotland and back but also west to Cornwall on the delightfully named *Night Riviera*. I did wonder, though, about those passengers for whom this challenging score did not conjure up such cherished memories.

Spean Bridge/Drochaid an Aonachain 20.08
Emergency Exits
In emergency, use hammer to break windows

Unsettlingly, I was already feeling sleepy by the time we reached Spean Bridge. The previous night, I had found myself in lowland Moniaive, a village boasting several music festivals, celebrity inhabitants and a cat called Zimmerman. It had been the day of the

At Night

referendum on Scottish independence and at least one of the village pubs stayed open all night for what many in the progressive little community clearly hoped would be a celebration but which – when I poked my nose in at six – had the unmistakable appearance of a wake. I myself had been up until four, by which time it had become only too apparent which side had won. My 90 minutes of sleep were peppered with dreams of thwarted ambition.

It meant that I had a battle ahead of me if I was not to succumb to the hypnotic *di-dum-di-DUM* of the wheels. It made it no easier that I found myself obliged to turn off all the lights in order to see more than my reflection when I looked out of the window. Even so, it was already too dark to make out anything but the form of the countryside – and from Spean Bridge that form was mostly tree-shaped. This is former Commando country. The famous memorial to those elite forces is just a mile from the station and overlooks the terrain across which they trained during World War II. Many a violent raid and ruthless assault was first imagined among those tranquil hills, benign forests and guileless burns. I peered out onto a landscape where not a single light showed. I got the distinct impression that we were intruding and that once the gloaming had swallowed us up again, the wind would breathe a sigh of relief and the shell-shocked land would settle back into an uneasy peace once more.

Tulloch/An Tulach 20.26
1. Strike windows HARD in CORNER
to break glass
Penalty for improper use

There was something magnificently lonely and abandoned about Tulloch station, even at this relatively early hour. Its fiery lights blazed down on an empty bench stranded in a sea of tiny stones. On the way up to Fort William I'd noticed that many of these Highland stations are buried under what seems an absurdly thick carpet of gravel, presumably to prevent them from becoming ice rinks during the long winter months. On the way back down I was afforded every opportunity to study this phenomenon.

Of all trains, the sleeper is the least hurried. We stopped and we waited. No one alighted. No one boarded. Still we waited. True, we had 550 miles or so to travel but then we also had a full 12 hours in which to complete our odyssey. A meagre 45mph would do it. While we might duck below that on the tight curves and climbs of the West Highland Line, we could rattle along at 80 further south and even 100 if we were late and needed to make up time. So we waited. The angry mice were pacified, but a low grumbling throb deep within the train seemed to ask, 'Why are you in such a hurry to be in London anyway? You know what it does to you.' So we sat patiently while a freight train pulled in at the opposite platform. We sat patiently as it loitered. We sat patiently as it pulled out again. Of all trains, the sleeper is the least hurried.

It was only on leaving Tulloch that we turned south at last, smuggling ourselves along the River Treig and then the shore of its loch to pass between unseen mountains guarding the northern approaches to the high moor.

Rannoch/Raineach 21.05
To get help
Get help from the train staff OR
Get help from the lounge car

Sliding through Corrour, the highest railway station in Britain and arguably its most remote, we reached Rannoch. The moor, which extends from here to the west and south, and from which the station takes its name, is not a place to be caught out on at night. It is a dish of water held 1,000ft up in the air, a 50 square mile triangle of peat bogs and burns, of lochans and lochs surrounded by unhelpful mountains. In winter, much of that water freezes, rendering Rannoch Moor even more inhospitable to whatever human life might struggle across it. Not for nothing does Robert Louis Stevenson declare of Rannoch in his novel *Kidnapped*, 'A wearier looking desert a man never saw.'

Wildlife fares rather better here – this is home to the rare narrow-headed ant and the Rannoch rush, a plant found nowhere else in Britain. Despite its barren aspect – lost to me now in the moonless night – the peat deposits on the moor teem with so much life that the whole area is conserved for scientific study.

It is those same peat deposits that have all but kept restless humans at bay. Not a single road crosses the moor. A finger of tarmac edges in from the east only to come to an abrupt end at Rannoch station, chary of penetrating further. The surprisingly substantial station building and the even more surprising hotel nearby – it was built to house the West Highland line's engineers over a hundred years ago and has simply forgotten to die – represent the last outposts of civilisation for anyone taking on the moor from this direction. Those not heading across it by rail must necessarily strike out on foot, with one small youth hostel by Loch Ossian and a restaurant with rooms on the platform at Corrour providing the only shelter in the wilderness.

It's something of a miracle that this railway line exists at all. Those late Victorian engineers huddled together in what is now the Moor of Rannoch Hotel were obliged to float a snaking band of soil, ashes, brushwood and tree roots over the moor and, not without some misgivings, lay the tracks upon it. Furthermore, this major undertaking was but a small section of a 101-mile line stretching from the Firth of Clyde to Fort William, which, it is claimed, is the longest section of railway ever built at a single go. The enterprise took five years and the labours of 5,000 men.

I had seen something of the forsaken beauty of the moor in daylight and I shivered as I imagined having to blunder across it in the cold of night. As a consequence, my little cabin with its single bed smartly made up with sheets and blankets, its long mirror, its hangers for my clothes, its aquamarine night light, its little lever to control the temperature, its purple-patterned strip of carpet, its myriad signs telling me what to do in every possible situation, its sink with hot and cold running water and its little swag bag of complimentary toiletries felt deliciously cosy. I was spared the trials and tribulations of life out on the blasted inky moor. I'm a big fan of the outdoors and spend more time in it than is perhaps natural, but for once I was happy to be swaddled and cosseted.

Bridge of Orchy/Drochaid Urchaidh 21.40
If it is not possible to go for help,
you may have to pull the emergency stop

Upper Tyndrum/Taigh an Droma Uarach 21.57
To stop the train
Pull the Emergency Stop handle
above carriage window

Two more stations shagpile-thick with gravel. Jaundice-bright and Swiss-tidy, I could have eaten my dinner off any flat surface they presented. And so bare, untenanted, deserted. At Bridge of Orchy five silver bicycle stands offered not a single scratch to prove that mortal man once stood there. I had the fanciful notion that they were in fact a giant's toast rack and the gravel merely crumbs. This is what sleep deprivation will do to you if you allow it.

The bridge over the River Orchy is not one of General Wade's but is the work of his successor, Major Caulfeild, a man who, when he wasn't building military roads, spent his time correcting spellings of his name. He slung the bridge across the turbulent Orchy, chaotic with white water, in 1751, and so dealt the Jacobites another slap in the face.

Upper Tyndrum's waiting room is an Alpine cottage. It serves a tiny village, perhaps the smallest community in Britain to be blessed by a brace of railway stations. The older of the brothers, Tyndrum Lower – a name so much more lyrical than prosaic Lower Tyndrum – lurked somewhere in the murk below us. It stands guard on the Oban line, so we would not be bothering it tonight.

Crianlarich/A' Chrìon Làraich 22.14
If an exterior door is not shut
and the train is moving
– stop the train

Ardlui/Àird Laoigh 22.39
If you can see a fire
– stop the train

Arrochar and Tarbet/An Tairbeart 22.54
After pulling the emergency stop handle
get help from the train staff

The sight of a man sauntering up the platform at Crianlarich took me aback. He was the first person I'd seen on a station aside from railway officials since we left Fort William. Sadly, there were no such surprises to be had at Ardlui or Arrochar and Tarbet, something that I couldn't help thinking was an opportunity missed. There are thousands of villages in Britain and only a small proportion boast their own railway station. Of those only a handful enjoy a nocturnal service connecting them with such fleshpots as Preston and Warrington.

'Things would be different if I lived here,' I vowed. 'I would be constantly on the move, rolling out of my cottage and heading down to the station when honest folk are preparing for bed. I might not go as far as London or even Carlisle but I would certainly hop onto one of the seated carriages and jump off at Dalmuir, say, just because I could.'

What I would then do in Dalmuir to pass the time until the first train back (the sleeper up from London) rolled in at 06.03 was neither here nor there. What mattered was the doing of it.

'If you have to ask why, you have no soul,' I would respond to my critics, of whom there are many.

And so ended the reverie.

As I stared blankly out into the night, seeing little but variations of dark grey as we trundled serenely along, the stations at which we stopped took on the nature of stars into whose brightly lit core I blinked until my eyes adjusted to their brilliance. They effused a striking calm. Unpeopled, they became Zen gardens, the patterns of their bricks and tiles the only busy thing about them. Few were adorned with much in the way of plant life yet there was something strangely soothing in their sterility. As the night wore on and I imagined more and more of my fellow travellers falling asleep or at least lolling about on their beds with the blinds down, ears plugged against the angry mice, I felt I was looking out onto a secret world. The long tranches of countryside, made anonymous by the darkness, were codes I could not break. The stations, however, were a different matter. Though enigmatic, they invited me to examine their every line, their every shadow, willing me to discover their hidden meaning as if they were Egyptian tombs and their arcane signs and symbols hieroglyphs.

It's fitting that Arrochar and Tarbet take equal custody of their railway station because they are villages that have long been thought of as twins. Arrochar watches over the head of Loch Long, which eventually gives on to the sea, while Tarbet does similar duty two miles to the east on the shores of Loch Lomond. Between Ardlui and Tarbet I pushed my head against the window and cupped my hands around my temples in order to take in this mighty benighted loch. My efforts were rewarded with a vast darkness, as if I had gone blind, which was how I knew it was out there.

The cord that ties Arrochar and Tarbet is the slender valley of the Tarbet Burn. For many centuries sailors and fishermen moved from one loch to the other by dragging their boats along this low-lying cut through the hills. This arduous practice is immortalised in the Gaelic *An Tairbeart*, which has come to signify an isthmus but literally means *draw-boat*.

Local mariners are not the only ones to have taken advantage of this topographical quirk. In 1263, long after the golden era of Viking raids had passed, a band of Norsemen, Manxmen and Hebrideans broke off from a larger Viking fleet and cheekily sailed up Loch Long. They hauled their 60 longships from Arrochar to Tarbet on wooden rollers and proceeded to pillage their way up and down Loch Lomond. They got their comeuppance a few days later, though. After rejoining the mother fleet in Rothesay Bay a storm drove them ashore at Largs where the troops of Alexander II of Scotland despatched them almost to a man. It was the last time the Vikings attempted an incursion into Britain.

Nowadays there's not so much call for dragging boats through the valley. The A83 threads itself from end to end, making the railway line leap over it in order to obtain the eastern shore of Loch Long and so head south towards Craggan Hill.

Garelochhead/Ceann a' Gheàrrloch 23.18
Escape
The safest place in most
emergencies is on the train

The train dragged itself into Garelochhead as if it regretted ever having started the journey. Three and a half hours after leaving Fort William we had travelled a scant 90 miles. To put this into perspective, had this been a stage in the Tour de France, we'd have been dropped from the peloton by now. I confess, however, that I was beginning to enjoy this counter-cultural approach to travel. In China, the Shanghai maglev train whizzes passengers around at an astonishing 267mph, but has that really added to the sum of human happiness?

A young woman in red wearing a woolly hat boarded and took the cabin next to mine. There was about a minute's scuffling next door and then silence. She was clearly an old hand at this game. Whenever I get on a sleeper I'm far too excited just to dump my bags and go straight to bed. There's all the exploring to be done for a start: the fun to be had from opening things and lifting things and finding other things behind or underneath. On a sleeper from Paris to Barcelona I opened a door in my cabin to discover there was a whole private bathroom behind it, or at least a cupboard-sized room fitted with a loo and a shower. On this train the delights are more modest but I'm still just as thrilled about raising a section of the ledge by the window to reveal a basin and taps underneath as I was when I first saw this trick performed as a child travelling up to Scotland overnight with my mother.

The railway came to Garelochhead in 1894 and its arrival made it possible for wealthier citizens to travel daily into Glasgow to their places of work. Little did they know at the time but they were in the vanguard of what would become an army of British long-distance rail commuters – those men and women who, by necessity or choice, sacrifice huge chunks of their time on Earth in order to make a life in one place and a living in another many miles away.

After so much nothingness, the unexpected conglomeration of lights below us made humble Garelochhead seem like a city. Not far beyond, the huge naval base at Faslane – home to the nation's nuclear-armed submarine fleet – was skulking behind mountains of razor wire on the shore of Gare Loch. It is a strange life the crews of these submarines have chosen. They dive down into the depths of the oceans where they seal themselves in perpetual night. There they spend weeks at a time sitting in a tube knowing that, if they are ever called into action, it might not be worth ever leaving it.

Helensburgh Upper/Baile Eilidh Ard 23.44
Do NOT get off unless
told to by the staff. If in
danger it is safer to move
along the train

Dumbarton Central/
Dùn Breatann Meadhain 23.49
To escape if the door is
locked pull the green
ESCAPE handle then use
the outside handle

Between them, these two stations marked not the end of the journey, or even the beginning of the end, but they did, perhaps, signal the end of the beginning, for there could be no doubting now that we had exchanged the Highlands for lowland towns, satellites of the great Glasgow conurbation. The impenetrable night was suddenly pockmarked with lights. Helensburgh and Dumbarton may not be the cities that never sleep, but they are the towns that like to ensure their citizens can get home of an evening on reasonably illuminated streets.

Dalmuir/Dail Mhoire 23.59
To escape through a
window get a hammer
then smash the corner
of the window

Here we pass the witching hour. In my other life I get
off here and just hang about for six hours until the
northbound sleeper arrives. I'm not sure, on reflection,
how happy I am in that other life.

Westerton 00.08
Do not get off the train onto a track unless
instructed by the train staff

The screeching of brakes that drew us to a halt at
Westerton was soon followed by a flurry of activity
somewhat disproportionate to the size of the place, or
at least my estimation of the size of the place gauged
by the lights I had seen in the district. I discovered
only later that the passengers scurrying from further
up the train were probably intent on picking up the
last train to Glasgow, there being a service laid on to
connect with the sleeper. It was the last station en
route at which I witnessed any significant hustle and
bustle. Ours was otherwise a train of the insensible,
of pupae tucked away in cocoons, content to gather
strength until we emerged, full nerved, onto the streets
of London.

Edinburgh Waverley 01.15
Night Light
Dim Bright

At Edinburgh Waverley, the train was in trouble. I took my bicycle off, as requested by Redmayne, and was wheeling it down the platform when I came upon a couple of engineers struggling with the back door. They were evidently trying to get it open prior to coupling up with the portion that had come down from Aberdeen. Keen to extend my stay outside, even though this wasn't strictly *outside*, given the majestic roof that covers the station, I stopped to watch them. The senior engineer, a man in late middle age with a pate that gleamed beneath the station lights despite what looked suspiciously like a comb-over, was tackling the problem by calling upon his many years of experience. The junior engineer, a man who seemed barely out of his teens, looked on and learnt, occasionally communicating with the Aberdeen crew via a walkie-talkie. For five and then ten minutes the older man wrestled with the door, first from the outside and then from within and then from the outside again with the younger man within responding to commands called through a crack between the door and the frame, a crack that had grown no larger since the operation had begun. Eventually, all subtlety abandoned, brute force was employed. At once the door flew open.

The senior engineer gave a grunt that was half satisfaction and half frustration that he had wasted so much time calling upon his many years of experience. Still, nothing is ever truly wasted: he could add this to his many years of experience and the next time a conductor reported a jammed end door he could just say, 'Give it a good yank, mate,' and go back to his cup of tea.

I was told to pop my bike on at the very front of the train, just beyond Coach A. This door wouldn't open either, even when I gave it a good yank. Wondering if I could open it from inside, I walked back to the door of Coach A, a carriage with seats rather than cabins, and stepped on board. A young man followed me in. I don't think either of us were prepared for what we were about to see.

This was truly the Coach of the Damned. Almost every seat was taken and those that were not taken were home to limbs that rightly belonged on other seats. With very few exceptions, everyone was wearing the standard-issue dark blue blindfold presented to sleeper passengers. One man, sprawled as only a man can sprawl, had his mouth wide open but there issued not a sound from it. Indeed, he hardly seemed to breathe at all. With his blindfold covering half his face, he looked like a man who had just been executed by firing squad. But much worse than this was the rebarbative funk into which we walked as soon as we entered the carriage. We were not even half way into the night and yet the less than sweet fragrance of bodies was so overwhelming I had to repress a gag.

This was a world I recognised only too well. I have taken too many nocturnal bus journeys across Mexico with my knees in my chin and someone else's wet moustache on my shoulder. I have attempted sleep on the floor of storm-tossed ferries lurching across the North Sea with schoolchildren throwing up inches from my head. I have sunk to Promethean depths of misery in the pursuit of cheap overnight travel and I have not emerged unscathed.

I turned round and caught the horrified expression on the face of the young man who had followed me in. His eyes flicked desperately around the carriage in search of some sort of sanctuary. There was just one seat that contained neither body nor extraneous appendage and he sat meekly down in it, legs together, arms folded in front of him, no doubt attempting to identify which of his sins was responsible for landing him here. He gave me an imploring look, shot through with wild incomprehension. He was a drowning mariner sinking beneath the waves and fixing his last hope of rescue upon a passing seabird.

I found I couldn't get through that way to the door I needed to open so I turned around and strode back through Coach A. I jumped out onto the platform and exhaled. Eventually someone in uniform came to unlock the door and I hauled my bike on.

'We're leaving in a moment so could you walk to your cabin through the train please, sir?' I heard the uniform say.

I took a deep breath and walked through Coach A for a third time, half expecting to see the young man being devoured alive by members of the undead. I marched on as fast as I could while stepping carefully through the mangrove tangle of limbs in the aisle. I did not look back.

Carlisle 03.22
Fire Alarm
The alarm is a continuous loud high pitched note. The same note sounded intermittently indicates a fire alarm fault

Carlisle station looked pristine and shiny, as if it were expecting a visit from royalty or perhaps the General Secretary of the United Nations. It's a station I know well and my mind wandered through all the happy times I'd got off here on my way to unfashionable but rather lovely bits of Cumbria. In my experience, it is always about to rain in Carlisle but rarely carries out its threat beyond some peremptory spitting.

For a change of scene – and, if I'm honest, to check for telltale spots of rain on the windows – I took a stroll up and down the narrow corridor. Passing all the little doors, it was impossible not to imagine

Hercule Poirot waddling towards me, albeit that the carriages of the Orient Express necessarily lacked the glamour of a British Rail Workshops-built Mark 3A sleeper car. As far as I have been able to ascertain, British sleeper trains are not hotbeds of crime and certainly not frequent scenes of murder, which is cheering. Indeed, when it comes to railway crimes that took place in Britain at night, there's only one that springs readily to mind and that didn't even involve a sleeper train.

The night mail service from Glasgow to London had been running without let or hindrance more or less every night for 125 years when a false red light brought it to a halt near Bridego Railway Bridge in Buckinghamshire. It was 3am on 8 August 1963. The train had made its usual stops at Carstairs, Carlisle, Preston, Warrington, Crewe, Tamworth and Rugby as around 70 on-board staff busily sorted through mail, flicking thousands of cards and letters onto little wooden racks, just like you see on the film *Night Mail*, only W H Auden's train was heading the other way, from London to Glasgow.

What happened next is well known and is probably the only context now in which you will ever hear the word 'cosh'. After the coup, which netted around £2.5m, the 15-strong gang headed up by Bruce Reynolds (Ronnie Biggs was but a minor figure) holed up in a remote farmhouse. Although the robbery went more or less smoothly, their plans were undone when the man commissioned to burn the farmhouse down after they had left failed to do so. Incriminating evidence that should have gone up in smoke thus fell into the hands of the police.

The Great Train Robbery has rather overshadowed a similarly spectacular raid on an overnight train that occurred the century before. On 15 May 1855, William Pierce and Edward Agar, with the help of a couple of railway employees, stole £15,000-worth of gold bullion and coin from a train travelling from London Bridge to Folkestone. The gang only came to grief when Agar was arrested for a wholly separate crime and condemned to deportation. Sitting glumly in a prison ship at Portland he learnt from his lover, Fanny Kay, that his associates had kept some of the share of the takings that they had promised to pass on to her. Before you could say 'honour among thieves' he was turning Queen's evidence.

It's interesting to note that while these two nocturnal robberies were carried off successfully, in both cases the downfall of the perpetrators came about because of a relatively trifling error after the fact. If you are planning your own raid on a train after hours, it might be wise to take note of this and learn from the mistakes of Pierce and Reynolds. You can give up all thoughts of recreating the Great Train Robbery though – the Royal Mail ran its last overnight mail sorting train back in 2004.

Warrington Bank Quay 05.13
Alarm incendie
L'alarme est donnee par un son
aigu puissant et continu.
Tout son intermittent denote
un defaut de l'alarme incendie

I was so tired by the time we eased ourselves into Warrington Bank Quay that all I could think about was that if the General Secretary of the United Nations ever visited, they could mark the occasion by adding the word 'Moon' to the end of the station name, possibly permanently. My ill-marshalled brain found this thought so hilarious that it made a note to ask the relevant authorities to make this happen within my lifetime.

The timetable had stated that after Glasgow Queen Street, which, of course, we didn't trouble with our presence, we would be stopping at Preston and then Crewe. Unless I helped myself unawares to two rations of micro-sleep at these stations, I would contend that we called at neither one nor the other. Perhaps this is why we stopped at Warrington, which is halfway between the two but still a challenging 30-mile walk to either.

London Euston 07.48
Feuerwarnung
Die Feuerwarnung wird durch
einen anhaltenden lauten
hohen Ton gegeben. Der gleiche
doch mit Unterbrechungen
abgegebene Ton zeigt den Ausfall
des Feuerwarnsystems an

Passing from the industrial northwest to the Midlands in the aquamarine haze of my cabin's night light, England rushed past the window intent on mesmerising me. Gone was the chuntering and maundering that characterised the Scottish leg of the journey – now we were really hitting our straps. It's true that we were not travelling as fast as would a daytime train on this section but at least one benchmark of rapidity had been achieved: we were speeding too fast through stations for their names to be legible. Thus, as I sat on my bed fighting gravity for control over my eyelids, I had little idea of precisely where we were for what seemed like aeons. The nation was measured out, not in coffee spoons, as T S Eliot would have it, but in blazes of light (cities), sparks of light (towns and villages) and darkness (countryside) with the occasional interruption by something that was none of these, such as an illuminated antenna or a motorway. This is probably what England would see if it were about to die and its nocturnal life flashed before its eyes.

By 6.15, the first rumours of morning began to spread about the land. At first they were very subtle: I began to notice that the contrast between town and country was not quite so great as it had been. Streetlights became less fierce. Then the black spaces burst into competing shades of dark grey, until suddenly I found it was possible to pick out an enchanting silver mist that was icing the hedgerows around a field.

Having watched morning blossom from a bud rather than greet it fully unfurled as I normally do, breakfast seemed perversely late when Redmayne dropped it in to me an hour later. The vegetarian cooked breakfast I had requested was almost food, with the very small lump of spinach requiring particular detective work before I could identify it with any certainty. I was glad of the reviving orange juice, however, as well as the pot of hot water into which I enthusiastically introduced a teabag with fatigue-clumsy fingers.

I looked up, slightly ashamed to have been so sniffy about my breakfast when so many people around the world – indeed, even here on this train – would be waking up to none. I discovered that we had slowed down, for it was possible to read that we were passing through Leighton Buzzard station. Any moment now we would be passing the spot where one of Bruce Reynolds' gang covered the green light with a glove, connected a 6-volt Ever Ready battery to the red light, and propelled himself and his comrades into folklore.

Redmayne, still his usual cheery self, came to pick up my breakfast tray and I asked him how his night had been.

'Same old, same old,' he replied with a wry smile. He shouldn't really have been here at all, he explained, but was covering a colleague's shift. Even though he switched between all five Caledonian Sleeper routes, he admitted that his working night was somewhat predictable. Like so many other jobs that seem glamorous and interesting to outsiders, the shine had come off rather quickly.

There is something to be said for same old same old, however. In Continental Europe, for example, in the face of stiff taxes and competition from budget airlines, sleeper train services are undergoing arguably the deepest cuts in their history and many workers like Redmayne are losing their jobs. It's news that deeply saddens me. Once upon a youth I whiled away a fortnight InterRailing around Western Europe, spending every single night in the seating carriage of a sleeper train because I could not afford accommodation. Each new morning I would be roused to bleary consciousness by the dawn in a fresh country. It's a journey I couldn't replicate now – mere fragments of it survive. By contrast, the Caledonian Sleeper's future appears secure. There are even some brand new coaches promised for 2018 which one would imagine will also sound the death knell for the angry mice.

I shall miss the old carriages when they go, though, for they've borne me south or north on many occasions and nowadays they're as sure a way of travelling three decades back in time as any 80s disco night. I'll miss the little lever by which you can adjust the sans serif temperature from max to min and back. I'll miss the royal blue button that lights up when you call the attendant, even though I've never been so bold as to use it. I'll miss the wonderful array of choices and combinations of lighting: berth light, main light, dim/bright, night light. I'll miss the blind that always takes me at least five goes before I get the hang of it. Most of all, I'll miss that secret hidden mysterious sink with the hot and cold running water – I do hope the new coaches have one of those.

It's raining on the rooftops and roads and offices and warehouses and retail outlets and workshops of north London and they are, every one of them, without exception, grey and grim. The Caledonian Sleeper does its best impression of a graceful swan dive as we enter Euston, and my spirits are lifted briefly by a steam engine chuffing past hauling some very fancy carriages. Once it has gone, I am left alone with an anonymous platform and I am reminded yet again that Euston is a station to leave from, not to arrive at.

At Night

Swiftly the platform fills up with passengers who look less weary than I feel. Beneficiaries of this little miracle of unconscious travel, they stride towards the ticket barriers dragging their wheeled luggage or advance at the more measured pace of the backpacker. I don't want to leave my cabin. The comfort I felt from its protecting walls as we crossed Rannoch Moor is amplified now as I consider that, given the choice between the two, I'd rather be wandering about among bogs and lochans than hacking my way across a city. The soft duvet of night has been ripped from my grasping hands and I'm plunged into day's cold shower. The hours of slothful rest are behind me and the time has come to be productive and useful – and if not productive or useful then at least busy. Busy busy busy. Put your sleepy lochans away and come immerse yourself in steel and concrete because the machine is hungry and if we do not feed it we will perish.

'There, I told you London would be like this,' says the low grumbling throb deep within the train. It coughs once and chokes itself into silence.

7

Bicycle

When William Harrison Ainsworth, in his novel *Rookwood*, had Dick Turpin ride from London to York in a single night he could not have known that it would set the highwayman on the road to becoming the romantic figure he is today. Even if one puts aside Turpin's nefarious deeds – for a while he belonged to a gang that routinely tortured victims in their own homes until they revealed where their valuables were hidden – he was not blessed with the physical beauty of an Adam Ant, which might otherwise have masked a multitude of sins.

'About 5 Feet 9 Inches high, brown Complexion, very much mark'd with the Small Pox, his Cheek-bones broad, his Face thinner towards the Bottom, his Visage short, pretty upright, and broad about the Shoulders.' Such is the unbecoming portrait sketched of him in the *Gentleman's Magazine* shortly after he had shot and killed a man who had attempted to apprehend him. It's a far cry from the fabled 'dandy highwayman so sick of easy fashion'.

At Night

Turpin was hanged in York at about the age of 34 on two counts of horse-stealing. A sensationalist account of his life rushed out in the aftermath of his execution did the perception of his character no favours. It would take Ainsworth and that 200-mile ride on a raven black mare to kick-start the process of rehabilitation that would lead to Turpin becoming a sort of Robin Hood of Epping Forest. From the facts we do know about him, I think it's fair to say that the concept of stealing from the rich to give to the poor is one that he would have found some difficulty grasping.

It just goes to show the power that an epic overnight journey can have on the imagination. Indeed, the breathless moonlit dash north would prove the only passage of Ainsworth's book that readers would really take to. None of the other fictionalised exploits in the novel have become part of the Dick Turpin legend, but everyone knows that Black Bess carried him to York and gloriously expired on arrival.

As a test of speed and endurance it is perhaps not quite of the same order, but when I told my friends that I was planning to cycle over a hundred miles from London to the Suffolk coast they were but mildly impressed. It was only when I added that I would be doing so overnight that their interest was piqued. There's clearly a mystique attached to leaving a place at nightfall and arriving at sunrise in a wholly new location many miles away. It's one of the reasons why 'driving through the night' is a familiar trope in pop songs – it's a shorthand way of conveying rebelliousness, freedom or commitment to a cause.

Like most species, we have come to expect that we shall wake up more or less where we fell asleep. We associate the night with being static, becalmed. We might toss and turn a bit, and some may even sleepwalk, but as a rule it is the one period in each 24-hour shift when our frenzied movements hither and yon come to a halt. Hence there is something indefinably sneaky about popping up somewhere in the morning at a location that bears little relation to the one we were inhabiting the night before. It is perhaps the nearest most of us come to performing a magic trick.

So it was with no small sense of anticipation that I cycled the couple of miles from my home to London Fields on my ancient Raleigh Winner. This is a bike that, when I was a youth, we would have called a racer. After all, it has a lightweight frame, relatively thin wheels and, all importantly, drop handlebars. Such has been the explosion in sales of proper racing bikes at prices that would have seemed staggering to my younger self (I know this because they seem staggering to my current self as well), bicycles like the Winner have been downgraded to the status of mere 'road bike', as if the idea of actually racing anybody on one was tantamount to a Formula 1 driver turning up at Monaco in a Ford Capri.

At Night

London Fields is a slightly scrubby park in Hackney, perhaps most famous nowadays for picnicking hipsters and roaming street gangs. This evening, however, it belonged to a multitude of fellow cyclists, here for the annual Dunwich Dynamo ride. The Dun Run, as its regulars call it, is Britain's original night ride. Much copied since it began in 1992, for a number of years it ran as a small pay-to-enter affair. In 1999 it was decided to make it an open event and it is now enjoyed by an estimated 2,000 riders.

That 'estimated' speaks volumes, for the Dun Run is the antithesis of highly regulated events such as the London Marathon. You don't have to book a place or pay any sort of registration fee. There are no sponsors, official or unofficial, and the only people likely to make any money out of it are the pubs and the pop-up stalls along the way that serve provender to hungry and thirsty riders.

There's not even a set route. There were apparently some maps showing a suggested route on sale for a pound at the start but I didn't see any. Asking around beforehand, I got the impression that most people simply followed the lights of whoever was in front of them – a strategy I decided to employ and which would only go wrong towards the end of the journey. Alternatively, you can navigate by the stars or devise a course based on road numbers that feature in the Fibonacci sequence if that's what rings your bell. The only rules laid down are that participants should not talk too loudly while going through villages in the wee small hours and not leave any litter anywhere.

The only concessions to anything that smacks of organisation are a feed stop around the halfway mark at a village hall and some return transport at Dunwich. At the former, volunteers serve up pasta, bread rolls and bananas. Endearingly, any profits made from the venture are put towards improving cycling facilities. The village hall at Great Waldingfield is usually pressed into service but this year the one at Sible Hedingham, a little earlier on the main route, is doing the honours. At Dunwich, coaches with trailers for bicycles are laid on by a group called Southwark Cyclists but there are always far more cyclists than places and waiting lists are reputedly lengthy.

This refreshing refusal to hem the event in with rules and regulations extended to the actual time it got underway. I arrived at the park just after 8pm – having read that riders set off between then and 9pm – only to discover that no one was making any moves to do so. It was an exceptionally balmy evening and there was a convivial summer-in-the-city atmosphere. Groups of lightly clad cyclists were chatting and laughing, chomping on energy bars or wolfing down bananas. Did I detect also a note of slightly forced jollity in the joking around that perhaps stemmed from an underlying nervousness about the challenge ahead? Or was that just me projecting?

At Night

Witnessing all the camaraderie I suddenly wished that I had managed to cajole a friend into coming along with me. I told myself that I had not done so because I wanted to immerse myself in the experience of cycling overnight rather than just chatting the hours away but now I wasn't so sure whether that wasn't an equally valid way of passing the night anyway. I looked around while waiting for the off but I couldn't see anyone else who was doing it on their own.

At around 8.15, without there having been any sort of announcement or signal, a few riders started to make their way north through the gates of the park. I hitched myself to the back of a group of a dozen or so male club cyclists. They rode expensive bikes, wore proper cycling gear and carried copious water bottles with them. Each had a small but bulging bag on his back. None of them, I could tell at a glance, had attached a single very weighty pannier to the back of his bike, giving it a rather alarming tilt to the left that would have to be countered by their leaning slightly to the right at all times.

I was also pretty confident that none of them had had a series of bike maintenance incidents in the previous few days that had led to them scurrying desperately around London a few hours beforehand in search of a new back wheel in what was now an apparently outdated and unpopular size. Nor would they have unwisely just purchased an eight-gear cassette which, no matter what frantic adjustments they made, offered up just two gears from which the chain would not immediately slip. Nor had they forgotten to bring along a reserve front lamp to back up the solar-powered light they had never tested to see if it would last all night. Nor had they just changed their pedals for an elderly pair, on the grounds that these were the only ones they owned that had toe clips, only to find once they had set off that the ball bearings inside them clicked and clonked and crunched with every revolution. Nor, and this was the most upsetting nor of the lot, would they have been forced to buy a wheel that was considerably thinner than the tyres or inner tubes they owned, with the result that, no matter how they tried, they couldn't stop the former from pinching the latter, a state of affairs that caused a large bulge near the valve. This meant that every time the protuberance hit the road there was a *berdomp* – a little jump, as though I had attached a Brazil nut to the tyre. As soon as I got going, the energy from this jolt sped from the wheel to the hub, up through the forks, into the saddle and thus into me about three times every second. I was very largely to blame for this frankly shambolic state of affairs, of course, though I was anxious to see if I could shift at least a little of the responsibility onto the shoulders of society.

How I yearned to be back on my old bike, an equally venerable but incredibly reliable Falcon

At Night

Oxford. I had travelled over 35,000 miles on it over the course of 14 years until one night just before the previous Christmas when I left my local pub to find the railings heart-sinkingly bare. Later inspection of CCTV footage in the days afterwards revealed that, having decided on an impromptu cheeky final round of halves with the friend I was with, we had left at 10.28. The bike was stolen at 10.26. The miscreant, who had been hanging around waiting for drinkers at outside tables to leave, had kept his face from the camera and was unidentifiable. For months I searched online and at places notorious for selling stolen bikes such as the Sunday market at Brick Lane, but all to no avail. Now, as I cycled out of the park, my chain *clunkTHUNKED* from one missed gear to the next, my pedals *clicked* and *clacked*, and my tyre *berdomp-berdomp-berdomped*. The combined soundscape gave the impression that I had created some infernal percussive instrument on which I was playing an experimental jazz piece. I did not think altogether kind thoughts towards the thief.

Initial progress was slow. Perhaps surprisingly, this had little to do with the state of my bike and was more a function of the labyrinthine route we were taking through the back streets of Hackney. Across tiny parks and churchyards we crawled and along an alleyway where we all got off and pushed. There was also an exceptional amount of traffic about, no doubt consisting of people coaxed out of their homes

204

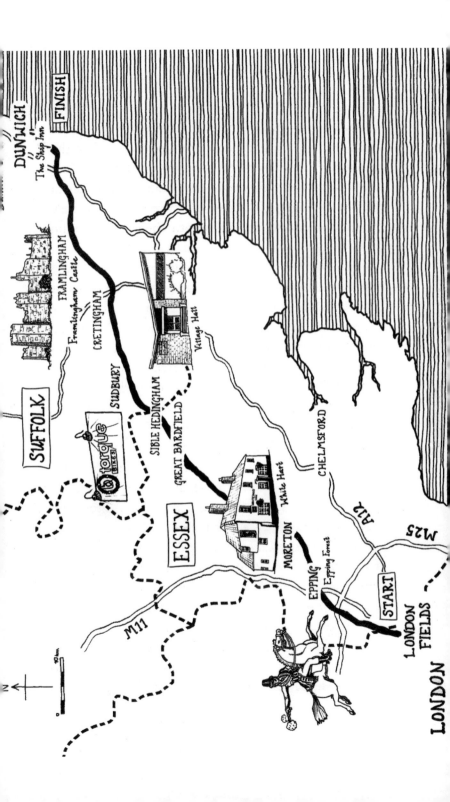

N

10 km

DUNWICH

FINISH

The Ship Inn

SUFFOLK

FRAMLINGHAM

Framlingham Castle

CRETINGHAM

SUDBURY

torque BIKES

Village Hall

SIBLE HEDINGHAM

GREAT BARDFIELD

ESSEX

White Hart

MORETON

CHELMSFORD

Epping Forest

EPPING

M11

A12

M25

START

LONDON FIELDS

LONDON

by the stifling humidity. After 10 minutes my speedo declared that we had done precisely one mile. With the night's venture clocking in at around 115 miles all told, at this rate we would not reach the beach at Dunwich until mid-afternoon. Furthermore, I could no longer stand the *berdomp-berdomp-berdomp*, so I pulled myself out of the stream of merry cyclists and spent a fruitless 15 minutes attempting to put matters right. Hot, sweaty and frustrated, I set off again, telling myself that I would just have to treat the night as an exercise in stoicism.

Back in the flow of bicycles and on more significant roads, things began to speed along a little and I was able to give the task ahead some thought. Although I am an inveterate cyclist, I had never cycled more than 80 miles in a single day, and that was a memory now ten years old. I had not done any training and my bike was a wreck. Added to this, the weather forecast had also looked unfriendly from about 2am onwards. Given that thousands of people have succeeded in getting themselves from London to Dunwich over the years – one of them on a penny farthing – it had never occurred to me that I might fail. Now I had visions of myself in the pouring rain wrestling with some irreparable bike part at three in the morning. Lost.

I tried to put these dismal thoughts to the back of my mind. 'It may be a long way,' I tried to reason, 'but there is barely a hill worthy of the name between here and the Suffolk coast. Also, it is not a race, so if I arrive at any time tomorrow I will have triumphed.' It began to spit with rain.

After 7 miles of crossing and recrossing the River Lea I reached Epping Forest. The atmosphere was still unreasonably humid and I was averaging a measly 10mph but the peloton, once glimmering and vast, was beginning to stretch out a bit which made the going easier. I was reminded that I was heading through one of Dick Turpin's favourite stamping grounds. One of his first escapades took place in the forest. Two years later, with a high price on his head, Turpin fled back here to hide. He no doubt judged that the thick woods would conceal him by day and the fear among the populace of bumping into ne'er-do-wells like himself would shield him by night. However, he was spotted by the eagle-eyed Thomas Morris, one of the forest keeper's servants, who tried to arrest him. Though armed with pistols, Morris was no match for Turpin, who gunned him down with his carbine.

Over the years I've been a frequent visitor to the 'People's Forest', so called because it was handed over to the nation's subjects by Queen Victoria. It's the first substantial belt of woodland beyond east London and a popular place for Londoners to escape to at the weekend. However, I had never really grasped just how big it is. Even with the settlements that have encroached upon it and boxed it in, its main tranche still stretches for over 6 miles from Chingford to Epping. When Turpin rode its winding paths it would have afforded him myriad opportunities to disappear into its depths, horse and all, especially under cover of night.

By the time I came bowling along Epping High Street, with a hundred miles to go, it was a quarter to ten and almost dark. Having seen precious little in terms of wildlife while crossing the forest, an urban bat raced around my head as I was passing a betting shop. I was now reduced to a single gear that worked but was strangely comforted by the fact that I had already seen half a dozen bicycles upside down by the side of the road while their owners mended punctures or made other running repairs. I was also pleased to note that there was a healthy proportion of riders who were dressed in street clothes as I was rather than in the go-faster Lycra beloved of club cyclists.

Epping is where I would say goodbye to the ghost of Dick Turpin. Two days after killing Thomas Morris, he was reportedly carrying out yet more highway robberies just outside the town. Whatever his faults, he cannot be accused of lacking chutzpah. A few weeks later he would change his name to John Palmer, head north to the East Riding of Yorkshire and become a horse thief, his final and fatal change of profession.

As the light faded and my looking became peering, I began to muse on my situation. 'I am a grown man and unafraid of the dark. I am not all that far from home and certainly far from alone, even if my interactions with fellow cyclists are restricted to quips and mutual words of encouragement, the latter usually directed towards me by someone with tree-trunk thighs flying past. I have a pannier packed with all manner of healthy snacks and a reviving flask of tea. I cycle at night several times a week. So why do I still feel an apprehension about the oncoming darkness?' Here I was, speeding up in order to cover as many miles as I could before night's portcullis came down.

I tried to determine what the source of this anxiety could possibly be. Of course, one obvious disadvantage about cycling in the dark, no matter how good a light you have, is that it's harder to see and avoid pot-holes. I was pretty sure that it wasn't just that though. I didn't particularly fear getting lost, even though a glance at the traditional Dun Run route beforehand showed me we would be weaving across country on minor roads virtually the whole way. So far, however, there had always been plenty of cyclists to follow, and even if I did get separated from the pack, I reckoned I couldn't go far wrong if I kept following my nose roughly northeast.

On reflection, and I can only speak for myself here, I think it may have had something to do with trespassing. The daytime has been our species' natural environment for most of our existence. It is only relatively recently that artificial light has pushed the boundaries of our day into the territory of the night. Meanwhile, many people around the world continue to live their lives entirely by the sun.

When I worked with a Q'eqchi' community in the Guatemalan jungle, the only sources of light they controlled aside from cooking fires were torches – which used batteries that they found expensive – and home-made rag lamps that burnt similarly pricey fuel that also had to be lugged in over many miles of muddy footpaths. As a result, the community retired to bed as one soon after dark and rose at the first glimmer of light in the morning sky. Since humans do not boast senses that are particularly well adapted to the dark, that was a more natural way of relating to the comings and goings of the sun, even if it was dictated by poverty.

Most of us, however, have never lived that way and it would seem absurd to us to imagine that our day should end simply because the sun happened to have disappeared over the horizon. I would suggest, though, that we are still merely interlopers in the land of the night, there under sufferance. Should we ever lose our ability as a species to bring our artificial sunlight across the border and into the night we shall be banished again to the daylight. Mind you, if there's ever a time when we can no longer make our own light, we'll probably have bigger problems to contend with than not being able to go out at night.

Perhaps I did have some atavistic sense rise up within me that I was leaving my natural environment and that I would have to fend for myself until the kind old sun returned. In the long unlit stretches of country lane that lay before me, all I had to protect myself as I *click-clack berdomped clankTHUNKED* and dusk turned to nightfall was a solitary bicycle light that might not have soaked up enough rays of the sun to keep the darkness at bay all night. O to have brought the sort of never-failing lamp that gives the Dunwich Dynamo its name. I would have to put my faith in the kindly flashing red lights of cyclists ahead of me to pull me through until dawn. I was not sure I could rely on them either since the miles were sure to play havoc with the turbid ebb and flow of riders until the stream disintegrated into fragments and the time would come when there were no lights ahead and no lights behind and the road and the sky would become one. Furthermore, I had not become acquainted with this particular night yet and I find such introductions difficult.

It was only after another 5 miles that I reached the countryside proper and encountered true darkness. Extraordinary though Epping Forest is, I never feel that it's genuinely rural. I know that may sound faintly ridiculous when describing a woodland that covers over 6,000 acres but for me there's still a sense of it having one foot in London, no matter that its northern reaches are in Essex. Now I had ventured at last beyond the houses and, to my right, on the far side of a night-blackened hedge, was the promise of an open field.

Then, all of a sudden, 'BANG!'

As if to celebrate my escape from London and its satellite towns, a huge red firework burst into a thousand brilliant fragments. I rolled into the village of Moreton in a haze of delicious-smelling cordite, a smell I have loved since I first smelt it as a child on Bonfire Night. Here I came across little knots of spectators shouting 'Well done!' and *'Allez! Allez!'* as my fellow cyclists and I trundled past. It felt mildly fraudulent to acknowledge these cries, having really come so little distance, and I felt ashamed of my clanking, clunking bike. It was only when I worked out that I had suffered the *berdomp* of my back tyre over 26,000 times by that stage (it's amazing what you can work out in your head when you have nothing to think about but following the red lights ahead of you) that I felt I probably had earned their plaudits after all.

Moreton, about 22 miles in, was also clearly the first milestone for a lot of riders. On the way I had passed occasional clusters of cyclists at petrol stations gorging on snacks and downing bottles of flavoured milk but here there were two pubs – the timber-framed White Hart Inn and the equally handsome Nag's Head – both dating from the 16th century and both too good to pass. Hundreds of cyclists stood about outside, replacing liquid lost to the thick warm air and chattering happily away about cycling and the journey ahead and about nothing in particular. I was pleased to see that, although many of them had soft drinks, there was still quite a good proportion clasping a pint of something stronger. 'These,' I mused, 'would be the people who would come to my aid at three in the morning when I was wrestling with some irreparable bike part in the pouring rain.' I only hoped they would not have drunk so much as to render them incapable of actually carrying out any service they might offer.

I was tempted to have a quick break here myself but I was mindful of the fact that I had barely scratched the surface of the ride. Furthermore, the uniform sludge-brown colour of the sky did not bode well. The Dun Run is always held on the Saturday night nearest to the July full moon but such thoughtful planning would prove vain tonight. Also, it does feel a bit sad to be drinking alone in a congregation composed of little companionable groups.

I felt vindicated in my decision to press on when, a few miles further along, and over three hours before it had been forecast, the heavens opened. I dragged my hi-vis waterproof from my pannier, lightening its load ever so slightly and thus very marginally decreasing the angle at which I had to lean. With my T-shirt now damp with rain as well as sweat, I hurriedly put the jacket on. This made the rain stop. I didn't like to tempt fate at first by taking it off again but after a quarter of an hour I had to if only to prevent myself from melting.

There followed a stretch in which I kept coming across roads that were not merely newly wet but strewn with puddles. Though I had been subjected to a short downpour, I had missed its evidently more brutal brother's visit to these parts. A few weeks later I watched a video a fellow rider had posted on the internet and was astonished to see that he had apparently spent hour after hour getting soaked, having been unfortunate enough to travel at the same speed and in the same direction as the rain clouds. By contrast, I spent the night following in their wake – only occasionally close enough to fly through a thick curtain of mist – until they withered away.

Miles of emptiness ensued, punctuated by the occasional clutch of houses. Then suddenly a cry went up:

'Tea! Coffee! Toilet! Feed station!'

I had blundered into a village. I had become so mesmerised by the unfolding blank road and the ever-retreating ever-replenishing pool of flashing red lights that I had not even registered its name. I stopped, not because I particularly wanted to rest, eat or drink but more because I felt an urgent desire to investigate what a feed station looked like. I found someone barbecuing beef burgers and sausages under a tarpaulin. His clients were perched on low garden walls outside, for it was still warm despite the rain. In a room that did not look as if it were always a café, a dozen or so diners were sitting at little white tables eating for the sake of refuelling rather than for the sake of eating, as if our nation had learnt nothing from the French after all the years they had been our neighbours. There was a lot of banana-devouring going on as well. To be honest, I don't know what I had expected to see at a feed station and I soon lost interest. I used the loo, nodded to the man hunched over the barbecue, politely declined his offer of grilled processed meats, and hit the road.

It was near the village of Great Bardfield, with 70 miles still to go, that I became aware that my back brake was in some distress. Fortunately, I had little occasion to apply it, but where there were descents combined with bends or holes in the road, my one-bike orchestra added its own violin section. Sadly, it was capable of little more than staccato screeches brought forth by the unhappy meeting of metal brake casing and brand new and rather expensive metal wheel rim, the former steadily incising the latter with every new pull on the brake lever.

Great Bardfield itself proved a convivial place. I arrived just after midnight when I thought I was beginning to exhaust the supply of helpful riders to follow and was surprised to find the wide main street of the village brightly lit and throbbing with life. Hundreds of cyclists were strewn about the place, most of them, it appeared, quaffing pints. There was a good deal of *click-click-clicking* as riders walked about in the awkward bow-legged fashion universally adopted by those wearing cleats on the bottom of their shoes. These hook into the pedals, ensuring the cyclist benefits from pulling the pedals up as much as when pushing them down. Unfortunately, rather like a Manx shearwater's feet, though cleats work well in one environment, they're rather less successful in another, and there was a good deal of timorous shuffling about carried out by those portering full pints across the road to comrades. From one or two of the conversations I earwigged, it was apparent that some participants were treating the Dun Run as a sort of drawn-out pub crawl, downing a pint every hour or two as they came across a hostelry, many of which had extended their opening hours for the occasion.

Bicycles had flopped down everywhere like exhausted pit ponies. One couple rode up on a tandem smothered in red, green and blue lights – one of many cycles whose owners had made a real effort, decking them out like Christmas trees. A man on an apple-green stilt bicycle came sweeping through, perched on a saddle 6ft up in the air. Just in case there was a chance that anyone might not notice him, he announced his fleeting presence with a blast of distorted music ripping out of a speaker.

The Great Bardfield crowd was fairly typical of the event as a whole. Largely white, mainly in their 30s and 40s, with men outnumbering women by about two or three to one. Beards, I noticed, were very much *en vogue*, though having just grown one myself I was clearly part of the problem rather than the solution.

Although it hadn't yet occurred to me to start feeling sleepy – I have seldom gone to sleep before 2am for most of my adult life – I was beginning to feel physically tired, which was a little alarming with roughly two-thirds of the ride still to go. My toes had begun to hurt, possibly from all the extra effort they were having to put in on account of my non-cooperative pedals. Some worrying signs of cramp – not something I usually suffer from – had started to creep into my legs and the little shudder that passed into my saddle on every single one of the now 50,000 back-wheel revolutions had rather taken its toll as well. Fears that I might not actually make it to Dunwich were only forced out by the realisation that since it was too late to get myself to a railway station or to any sort of accommodation, I had no alternative but to get there. This was comforting, at least in the original sense of the word: the Romans used *confortare* to mean 'to encourage' or 'fortify'. When I was at school a teacher illustrated this by telling us that a centurion would 'comfort' his soldiers by prodding them in the back with a spear so that they might advance more enthusiastically into battle. Thus goaded, but with tremulous cadence slow, I set off again.

Some miles later I misinformed some Germans. I'm not proud of it and I didn't mean to do so but I fear that my error caused them some grief, or at least some esurience. A couple overtook me and asked me in perfect English but in unmistakably Germanic tones (all right, they could have been Swiss or Austrian but something in their Teutonic bearing told me they were not) if we had already passed the main feed stop at Sible Hedingham. I knew the village hall was located around the halfway point of the ride and, on seeing that I had ridden only about 50 miles and I had not seen it, I confidently stated that we had not. They thanked me and pushed briskly on ahead. I never saw them again. By the time I reached Sudbury 10 miles later it dawned on me that I had misled them, as a look at a map much later confirmed. I hope they did not hold it against me, for they were clearly carrying nothing with them and I do not recall seeing another place serving anything edible until well after dawn.

I can only hope that they stopped off at Torque Bikes in Sudbury for there they could at least have bought some high-energy foods – or 'hi-energy fuel' as their manufacturers so often insist on calling them. I nearly didn't stop there myself but the sheer joy of seeing a bicycle shop open at 1.30 in the morning, coupled with the prospect of another 55 miles of my bike conspiring against me on nearly every front imaginable, compelled me to enter. Inside there was a long queue of riders whose bikes had also failed to make it there in one piece. Several mechanics were working flat out to get them back on the road and, in a gesture typical of the big-heartedness of many an independent bicycle shop, they were giving their labour free. I spent the best part of an hour in the shop and by the time I came out my bike was almost unrecognisable. New brakes, new pedals, a new tyre and a new inner tube had all been fitted and the mechanic had even had a quick go at adjusting the gears so that at least some of them worked. This was something of a boon when I had been reduced to just one for most of the journey.

When I rode away, I felt like a king. Better than that, I felt like the meritocratically elected president of an equitable republic with a universally admired national cuisine and a cool flag. No, strike that: I felt like Dick Turpin, only not the real murdery thiefy torturey Dick Turpin but the fictionalised Dick Turpin with his progressive policy regarding the redistribution of wealth and his ability to ride 200 miles in a single night. Before Sudbury, I had begun to harbour visions of being forced to sleep under a hedge, my bike having fallen apart completely. Now, at a stroke, any concerns I had had about not finishing were banished. I sped away, suddenly full of vim and determined to be on the beach at Dunwich by six.

At Night

Three miles later, I got a puncture.

I'll spare you the details of my attempts to will this slowish puncture to remain slowish and the furious pumping and repumping of the tyre at shorter and shorter intervals. Eventually, I stopped by a large white house that was sitting on its own gazing out across the road into a void. The front of the house was illuminated by a powerful array of lights and was the first place for some distance that had offered me the chance to see what I was doing.

Despite the impression I might have given, I am usually reasonably adept at bicycle maintenance, at least when I get around to it. I even had a spare inner tube with me this time, so I did not have to rely on some Suffolkian version of Lee of Sherwood to come to my rescue. I removed the pannier, which was almost as heavy as when I started because I'd eaten precious few of the energy bars and bananas I had brought with me. I turned the bike over onto its saddle and had a long draught of tea. It was 4.15am and still quite dark, but it also was the most pleasant time of the night for the humidity had lifted and, although there was not a star to be seen in the sky, the threat of rain had lifted too. The air was fresh and sweet smelling and gossamer light. Other cyclists passed me in dribs and drabs but sometimes there were periods of five minutes or more in which the road was silent. Seeing my upturned bicycle, some riders called out as they passed, asking if I needed help. In hushed tones, lest I awaken any sleeping inhabitants of the house, I cheerily assured them I was on top of things. A cock crew from somewhere in the back garden and I became aware of the muffled mewing of a cat who was presumably observing me from behind one of the windows. I laid out on top of a low wall the tools I would need and, in an unhurried and deliberate fashion, I began the operation.

I had made a conscious decision that rather than get upset about the fact that I had managed to get a puncture so soon after having my bike entirely sorted out, I would enjoy the experience. I took pleasure in that first moment when the tyre gave in to the tyre lever and allowed itself to be hooked up and over the rim. I slid my fingers carefully around the inside of the tyre, breathing in the smell of the rubber plantation from which it came, or at least the factory in which it was moulded. Disappointingly, there were no shards of glass or thorns or sharp bits of metal thrusting their way through the tyre that I could remove with a satisfying *threeeeeep*. It had clearly been a hit-and-run job. I decided, therefore, to take pleasure from the fact that I had not sliced up my fingers in the search for the malefactor. The cat's mewing meanwhile became more insistent and less muted.

The exchange of inner tubes completed, the tyre returned to its rightful place – crucially without pinching anything this time – I attempted to reunite wheel with bicycle. I had not remembered that my new wheel and cassette were, between them, so wide that it now required a feat of Charles Atlas-like proportions to wrench the forks far enough apart for the wheel to be manhandled back into place. Even the strapping mechanic in the bike shop in Sudbury had been unable to do this unaided and had called upon me to assist him. We managed it after a struggle but I noticed the raised eyebrow he directed at my bike afterwards.

I took a deep breath and gave it a few goes, trying out different techniques each time and lamenting the fact that I had never got around to growing a couple of extra hands. When I found my stoic poise beginning to slip, I decided to flag someone down instead. No sooner had I made this resolution than a tortoiseshell cat suddenly appeared on top of the wall. Curiosity had got the better of her and she had come to see what a human was doing out and about at an hour that rightfully belonged to the cat and the cockerel. Having dismissed my upturned bike and detached wheel in a single derisive glance, she turned to me and miaowed loudly. I'm very much a cat person and needed no second invitation to begin making a fuss of her. It was only then, as she walked up and down along the wall purring profusely and nuzzling her head into me that I realised that dawn had arrived, though it was not yet 5am. The lights from the house had masked this transformation so well that by the time I was aware of it and looked behind me, the void was not only no longer a void but had become a field with trees beyond and features almost as perceptible to the eye as if it had been midday.

I had made it through the night and out the other end. I might be by the side of the road with my bicycle in one more piece than was required for locomotion but the mild anxiety I had felt as the darkness engulfed me had been unwarranted. True, it had left me once the night had begun in earnest but I still find it curious that I should have felt it at all since there is nothing in my experience to make me in the least bit fearful of things nocturnal. However, I suspect that it is a sensation I share with many others at dusk.

I might have made it successfully through to dawn but I had to remind myself that I was still far from Dunwich. I waved down the next cyclists who came along – a very friendly couple in their 60s who were clearly as fit as two Stradivari – and with a bit of brute force my bicycle was roadworthy again. Now my only difficulty lay in trying to convince the cat that she should not take my departure as a personal affront.

For the remainder of the ride it seemed to me as though I were passing through a land of dreams. I felt fine physically – the myriad complaints my body had made at Great Bardfield had mysteriously melted away over the course of the night. I also realised that I had not really been sleepy at any point. Instead, a kind of unreality set in. Although I was continuing on the same ride, it felt like I was starting a brand new one. Part of my mind, no doubt slightly befuddled by the lack of sleep, couldn't quite comprehend how it was that I came to be setting off on a trip across Suffolk quite so early in the morning.

After a journey all but devoid of signs of fauna, a fox and a family of breakfasting rabbits now showed themselves. By six, as I entered Cretingham, a tiny crossroads village that is more pub than anything else, a joysworth of magpies bounced across the road and the wood pigeons were in full throaty voice, their five-note song landing on the rooftops and tumbling down to earth. I have always associated their thick mournful call with a purple-grey colour, as if they were singing their feathers, and it seemed a fitting score to a world whose colours had yet to be awakened by the sun.

After miles of Suffolk roads I did not know, Framlingham seemed an old friend, though I had only visited it for the first time the previous year. I couldn't resist a peek at the town's singular castle – it was built with 13 towers but no central keep – but it seemed unusually out of sorts and bed-headed under the drab sky so I didn't tarry.

Fellow riders were becoming scarce but whenever I came to a junction there always seemed to be somebody I could follow. It was only when I began to close in on the finish that things started to go wrong, which was ironic since these were roads with which I had scraped acquaintance in the few years since my sister and brother-in-law had come to live nearby. I had latched onto a group of half a dozen riders who seemed to be confident about where they were going, a confidence which turned out to be misplaced on three separate occasions in quick succession. Still, it did mean that we got to know quite a few roads from both directions. We were saved from further ignominy by a growing stream of hardened cyclists who, having made it to Dunwich, were now heading back to London. I was both thankful for their unwitting help as guides and impressed by their willingness to take on a 230-mile ride. I was also secretly quite pleased that they all looked rather grim-faced as they sped by in the opposite direction.

Our little pack crossed the A12 a short distance to the south of Blythburgh. It reminded me that I was in the domain of yet another of Britain's spectral red-eyed canine beasts. On 4 August 1577, as a tremendous storm struck the Suffolk coast, the terrible hound of the marshes, Black Shuck, burst into Blythburgh's Church of the Most Holy Trinity. He attacked the parishioners within, killing a man and a boy, and only left when the steeple tumbled in through the roof. Scorch marks made by his paws can still be seen on the north door and there continue to be occasional sightings of the beast to this day.

The violent tale jarred with the rather floaty feel of this morning-after-the-night-before and was forgotten as soon as I entered Dunwich Forest, among whose trees gentle Dartmoor ponies roam. It was half past seven when I finally rolled into Dunwich, over 11 hours after I had left London Fields. I was beaten to the beach by two small teenage girls in floral clothes with daypacks on their backs. They rode in on fixies – single-speed fixed-wheel bikes – looking as fresh as if they'd just set out ten minutes beforehand from the next village. This put my own achievement somewhat into perspective.

Dunwich is now a rather fetching village of old and expensive-looking houses and a population numbering fewer than a hundred. It's hard to believe that this was once the capital of East Anglia, a port that rivalled London in size and importance. Its undoing was a great storm surge that struck on New Year's Day 1286, sweeping huge parts of the town into the sea. Further mighty surges the following year sounded the death knell for Dunwich as a port of any stature and slowly but surely the sea has clawed away almost everything that stood here. The city that once boasted a church for every week of the year now makes do with just one, and that was built by the Victorians.

It must please the ghosts of the old place to see this former powerhouse of the east teeming with life once more. The large car park behind the beach was packed with slightly dazed yet jubilant cyclists. They formed gargantuan snaking queues at whose head was the promise of some form of refreshment, or pushed their bikes towards coaches that were waiting to take them back to London.

I forged my way through the crowd to find the beach was even more densely populated. It resembled one of those die-in protests or a scene from a public information film in which a nuclear bomb has just exploded, only with added bikes. Exhausted cyclists, some captured at last by sleep, were splayed out in all directions, distillations of triumph and dissolution, too spent even to wish that the beach were made of sand and not armoured with bumpy, unyielding shingle. However, a few doughty folk were keeping alive the Dun Run tradition of a dip in the sea. They effected a good simulacrum of people having fun despite their initial squeals and anguished yelps but the grating roar of pebbles and the dismal grey of the North Sea did little to tempt me to follow their example.

I slipped away to the Ship Inn, where a sign proudly proclaimed that it had been open since 5am, and stood outside supping the earliest pint of cider I think I have ever had. At midnight I would have been glad of its reviving coolness. By day, its icy bubbles

At Night

stung the back of my throat like eager thorns piercing a worn-out tyre. I put down the glass, mounted my troublesome steed, and rode out of the village into the sun-blanched day.

8

Boots

Writing in 1859 for the weekly journal *All the Year Round*, Charles Dickens, the pre-eminent novelist of his era, shared the following confidence:

> *Some years ago, a temporary inability to sleep, referable to a distressing impression, caused me to walk about the streets all night, for a series of several nights. The disorder might have taken a long time to conquer, if it had been faintly experimented on in bed; but, it was soon defeated by the brisk treatment of getting up directly after lying down, and going out, and coming home tired at sunrise.*

Such was the opening gambit of an essay detailing Dickens' nocturnal wanderings about London in search of sleep. It might be more accurate to say that the storyteller, newspaper editor and sometime parliamentary correspondent was in search of company. In the piece, he writes of seeking out companionship with mongers at Billingsgate fish market, with fruit-

and-veg traders at Covent Garden, with piemen, with hot-potato men, at railway stations – wherever two or three are gathered together, he is eager to make himself a third or a fourth. He even remarks that 'when a church clock strikes...it may be at first mistaken for company', which feels like something of a projection. He makes only one exception to this rule of general gregariousness. No doubt with his middle-class readers' strait-laced sensibilities in mind, he emphasises that he was never so badly in need of company that he took comfort from women of the night or in the consoling insensibility of the opium den. 'I knew well enough where to find Vice and Misfortune of all kinds, if I had chosen,' he avers, 'but they were put out of sight.'

The clean-living Dickens never lets us in on the secret as to the nature of the 'distressing impression' that had kept him from sleep, but it's not difficult to imagine that the London of his day could have furnished him with plenty of unpleasant sights to haunt him when he closed his eyes of a night.

Over 150 years after he took his self-prescribed cure for insomnia, it's a surprisingly simple task to reconstruct the walk he describes in his essay. His route is, in all likelihood, an amalgam of various of his nocturnal wanderings, pieced together for the sake of literary comeliness, but it works very well as a night walk, taking in many significant landmarks in a big loop through central London.

The author of *Hard Times* undertook these urban rambles in March, when the weather was 'damp, cloudy, and cold'. Perhaps understandably even the ravages of insomnia couldn't force him to spend the whole night out in these conditions. By his own admission, five hours was all he felt he could endure. Calculating that the sun rose around 5.30am – which is a shade optimistic for March – he therefore left home at half past midnight in order that he might have the satisfaction of making it through till dawn.

By contrast, I headed out to follow Dickens' trail through the capital in January, before even the snowdrops had bloomed. To replicate his experience as closely as possible I thus set out a little after 2.15am, which would allow me to witness the dawning of the new day five hours later in the approved manner. Though my particular night did not promise to be either damp or cloudy, it would at least make up for these omissions by being cold. The forecast predicted a temperature of 0°C which would fall to a bracing -2°C as the night progressed. Undaunted, I wrapped up warmly, turned off the lights, and stepped outside.

Dickens was a prodigious walker whether by daylight or moonshine. An occasional actor, he memorised his entire leading role in *The Frozen Deep*, a play written by his good friend and protégé Wilkie Collins, during a 20-mile walk that took in Finchley, Neasden and Willesden. I confess that these are not parts of London I readily associate with Dickens. For me, he inhabits the world of the *gwarn, mister, gi's yer apple core to eat* street urchin, which can only mean one place: the East End. I realise that this exposes me as a man who has dabbled with only the most popular sections of the Dickens canon but so be it. If God had intended us to read all the classics he'd have made sure there were a lot fewer of them. It meant at least that I felt in a thoroughly Dickens-like frame of mind as I began my walk through the streets of Bethnal Green.

It was a surreal start to the night because no sooner had I left my door than I was confronted by the sight of two young men, one of whom was manhandling some sort of very large metal frame while the other had perched a chair on his head and was berating his friend that he had 'broken that thing already'. The friend persisted in his attempts to carry the unhappy frame, despite the attentions of alcohol upon his body, so one can only imagine that the plans he had hatched for its future were of some moment.

This coupling proved to be an anomaly because almost everyone else I saw as I marched west through Whitechapel and on to Aldgate was on

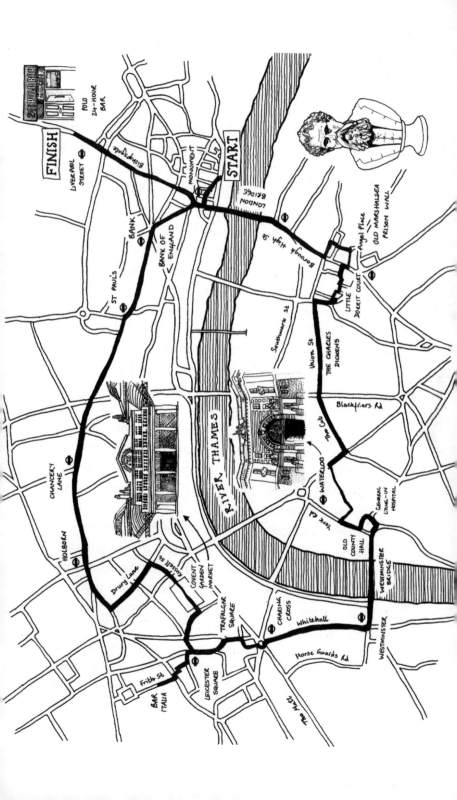

their own, typically with their head down and a sense of purpose to their gait that had been steeled by thoughts of a warm bed. Content that at least my lonely walk was in keeping with the times, I passed a brace of chicken emporia, one of which was still open and blazed with light of eye-aching intensity but was museum empty. The sole employee stared fixedly out into the street, the first man ever to have reached a state of Nirvana via a route of unalloyed boredom.

Further along to my left was the famous bust – famous locally at least – of William Booth, founder of The Salvation Army. A minute or two later I arrived at a hostel for the homeless that bears his name. Inside, a man wearing many layers of clothes was talking with the receptionist. As one might expect, Dickens encounters many homeless people on his way around London. He prefers the word *houseless* and, for the time that he's out pounding the streets, counts himself among their number. This might seem presumptuous in anyone else, but there's something so obviously sincere in his identification with the spirit of *houselessness* that he can just about get away with it. It also helps that there are few people in history who can claim to have matched him when it comes to bringing the plight of the downtrodden to the attention of the wider world.

A short distance from the north end of London Bridge, I arrived at last at a point on Dickens' loop around London. It was here that he visited Billingsgate fish market in his endless quest for nocturnal companionship. He was disappointed to find that he'd mis-timed his call and that the market had yet to open. He'd be even more disappointed were he to return today because Billingsgate has moved to a rather soulless location away to the east where it stands beside a trunk road at the edge of the regenerated Docklands. It is still open to the public, however, and from 4am on trading days anyone can wander in and mingle with the merchants, porters and fish buyers.

There is, as might be expected, something of a fishy tang to the air that does not encourage lingerers and the new premises consist of an exceptionally high-roofed metal box that exudes all the natural charm and atmosphere of an industrial warehouse. Fortunately, the old market building is still with us to remind us that not all mercantile architecture need be so determinedly utilitarian. Overlooking the Thames, its 11 high arches, yellow brick frontage and curving roof give it the look of a venerable Parisian railway terminus and it is tempting to imagine Dickens standing outside it looking forlornly at his watch. That would be a mistake, however, for this is not the building he knew but a confection constructed by Sir Horace Jones shortly after the author's death. The original market was, if anything, an even more stylish affair: it was blessed with a greater number of arches and sported a striking Italianate tower that must have given the riverside more the feel of sunny Florence than smoky London.

From here, Dickens crossed the river and made his way west across town. I had intended to do the same until it occurred to me, just as I was approaching London Bridge, that if I did so I would be unlikely to reach a particular coffee bar in Soho before it shut at 5am. Bar Italia never saw the patronage of Charles Dickens, having only been in existence since 1949. However, the café, which used to open all night and was immortalised in song by the 1990s Britpop band Pulp, provided a fitting modern-day equivalent to the cheap eateries the novelist used to frequent on his nightly rounds. If I found myself in need of human interaction then I was sure that the denizens of Bar Italia – a famously raffish crowd – would supply it. I therefore decided to follow Dickens' route in reverse, taking in the sights to the north of the river first, which I estimated would see me homing in on Soho an hour or so before the coffee bar was due to close.

I found myself heading up towards the Bank of England. Dickens makes only a passing reference to the Old Lady of Threadneedle Street, asking rather waspishly, 'Is there any haunting of the Bank Parlour, by the remorseful souls of old directors…?'

The social reformer wasn't against banks *per se* – after all, he and Angela Burdett-Coutts of Coutts

Bank collaborated in the founding of a home that enabled prostitutes to get off the streets – but he was often scathing in his judgement of those who manipulated the strings of the economy to the detriment of ordinary working people. It's a charge that is still being made, of course. Indeed, in the wake of the 2008 global financial collapse, the area in front of the Bank of England's grandiloquent portico drew demonstrators with conspicuously similar grievances to those of Dickens.

All was peaceful tonight though. Only the buses disturbed the calm, drawing to a halt and puttering impatiently at one of the many traffic lights that bring order to the eight roads that converge here. The major difference between my own experience of the place and that of Dickens was the light. In his time, this part of town was illuminated by the dim flickering of gas lamps. The streetlights installed in the area today are so powerful that they effectively turn night-time into day. In its defence it should be said that Bank is by no means the only part of London that suffers this perpetual daylight. Virtually my entire route from London Bridge to Leicester Square was bathed in artificial light. I was aware before I left home, of course, that the streets would be lit but I had never really considered just how absurdly bright so much of London is kept through the long hours of the night. It was effectively daytime but with the sky turned off. Ordinarily I wouldn't have given it a second thought but I had spent so much time out at night in the preceding months that there were certain things I had come to expect from that time of day, and one of these was darkness. Wherever I had been in Britain, the absence or near absence of light had brought with it an obvious sense of the night. Here, the only indications of it were a dearth of people and traffic, the 'N' prefix to the bus numbers, and the staggering sight of the steps of St Paul's entirely shorn of tourists.

In 1843, Dickens informed a friend that he had sketched out *A Christmas Carol* while walking 'the black streets of London, 15 and 20 miles, many a night when all the sober folks had gone to bed'. He'd be hard pressed to find 15 to 20 miles of darkened streets in the capital today. On the upside, from what I had witnessed thus far, he'd have plenty of time to ponder future novels free of the distraction of human interaction. It wasn't just along Whitechapel that solo wayfarers predominated. Nearly everyone I had seen since then was alone, intent on getting somewhere else and often wearing headphones into the bargain. The only groups of people I'd come across had been construction workers in hi-vis jackets fresh up from the bowels of the Earth. They smoked their cigarettes with a fevered intensity before stubbing them out and heading back down to nudge London's bold new £15bn east–west railway line a little further along.

not looking to see if they were displaying any of my books, though I was obviously looking to see if they were displaying any of my books. They weren't, and I pretended not to care. It could have been worse: they might have been displaying books written by my friends.

Dropping south down Drury Lane and into Russell Street, the side of the Theatre Royal was marked by a floodlit pavement flanked on one side by bright white colonnades and on the other by posters for the musical *Charlie and the Chocolate Factory*. In case that did not appeal, I only had to cross the road to the considerably more modest Fortune to be chilled by *The Woman in Black*, Susan Hill's hugely popular gothic horror story. Both theatres were barred to me now, of course. Their audiences would have streamed out – babbling happily of Oompa-Loompas or perhaps a little white about the gills, depending on the show they had chosen – and dispersed into the London night many hours ago. The doors were locked to all comers and would not be unlocked again until the respective box offices sprang back into life.

Theatre security was evidently a little more relaxed in Dickens' day. He tells of entering a playhouse (though he is careful not to name it) where, 'With a dim lantern in my hand, I groped my well-known way to the stage and looked over the orchestra – which was like a great grave dug for a time of pestilence –

into the void beyond... Methought I felt much as a diver might, at the bottom of the sea.'

I envied him his easy access. There's something rather thrilling about a vacant and darkened theatre. The freedom to roam about the auditorium at will, sit in a box and pretend you can afford it, or career up to the gods and peer down over the cliff face down into the stalls is rather intoxicating. Then there's that sense of expectation one gets from seeing an empty stage. Here is a space in which anything could happen, where dreams and nightmares are played out, a place where actors walk the tightrope with only the shaming prompt for a safety net.

It was fitting therefore that my next port of call should be Covent Garden, for it was here that Dickens came very close to becoming an actor. At the age of 20 he was invited to audition at the Theatre Royal by manager George Bartley and actor Charles Kemble. He took a great deal of time and trouble over the piece he was to present: something in the style of the then popular comic actor Charles Mathews. However, before he was due to perform, he contracted a cold and decided to pull out.

Although Dickens was to dabble with acting later on in life and his mesmerising readings of his own books drew in sell-out crowds, the moment had passed. The following year he sent his first story to the *Monthly Magazine* and his course through life was set. Fans of Dickens' work might ponder, the next time they bemoan that they are coming down with a cold, that if it hadn't been for the pesky rhinovirus or one of its equally noxious cousins, there would almost certainly be no Uriah Heep, no Thomas Gradgrind, no Mr Fezziwig, and no Pip to be threatened by Magwitch in a graveyard on the marshes.

Just as its predecessor had done in 1809, the Theatre Royal burnt down in 1856, 24 years after Dickens nearly auditioned there. Its replacement became the Royal Opera House, built to resemble a Doric temple transplanted from Ancient Greece. When I passed it, its vast white bulk with its six white columns topped by an unadorned white pediment actually blended in rather well with the old market at Covent Garden. This latter is a spotlessly clean and sanitised version of the former fruit-and-veg bazaar that stood here until the 1970s. Its business now is selling overpriced goods and coffee to tourists from its bijou shops and cafés. It was strange to see what I have always thought was a perpetually bustling space so tranquil. Even the living statues had gone home to clean the paint from their faces and rub some feeling back into their limbs. A lone security guard idled through the market square while another man swept the ground with a wide broom.

This was all a far cry from the market Dickens had cherished on account of it being 'as good as a party' in the early hours of the morning. At least the pitiful spectacle of homeless barefoot children driven by hunger to steal from the stalls is also a thing of the past hereabouts. The homeless outside the Apple Store, as far as I could tell from the proportions of the six sleeping bags I came across, were all filled by adults, though it doesn't take a Mother Teresa to be unsettled by the sight of such destitution in the doorway of a shop owned by the second most profitable company on the planet.

The environs of Leicester Square provided the first signs of real life in the city. A glass-fronted café advertising an unlikely special of 'FISH & CHIPS and FALAFEL' was humming with a youngish crowd. The scene was warm and inviting and I would have joined them myself had I not been keen to keep my date with Bar Italia.

Leicester Square itself was to prove not quite so beguiling. A bouncer rummaged through the bag of a spindly wild-eyed chap at the door of a casino; a group of men joked about outside a tawdry slot machine place; a couple of policemen chatted with three young women outside a darkened Pizza Hut. Some drunk people toddled on legs they could no longer wholly trust. It struck me then that there are similarities between being sleep-deprived and inebriated. There's often a slight nausea, a tendency to clumsiness, a dullness of mind, and, in my case at least, a difficulty putting together a coherent sentence.

These observations duly made, I wasted no more time there. It had already gone 4 o'clock and I wanted to get my fill of Bar Italia and its burghers before it closed at 5am.

On my way, down Little Newport Street, I encountered the first houseless people who had not taken to their sleeping bags. A middle-aged woman with an orange blanket wrapped around her and a cigarette angled precariously out of the corner of her mouth was giving lucid and confident directions to a young man. It was only her slightly slurred diction that gave away the fact that she had had a drink or two to keep out the cold. 'Can you spare some change, please?' she asked the man after she had made sure that he had understood exactly where he needed to go. He couldn't. Shortly afterwards I was asked the same question, though a shade more aggressively, by a man with very few front teeth, and then by a young man with a pustule-stricken face. I'm afraid I turned them both down.

I used to give to homeless people a lot more than I do now. I suppose I always knew deep down that tales of money needed for the proverbial 'cup of tea' or for buses to places where they could bed down at a friend's might not always be strictly true, and, even if true, those who told them might find the temptation to spend whatever I gave them on something that might not ultimately do them much good just too overwhelming. Pleas from charities who help rough sleepers that they could do more good with whatever money I could spare led me to harden my heart to requests from the homeless themselves.

However, I happened to be in Spitalfields, a once almost derelict but now notoriously trendy part of east London, one particularly frosty night last winter when I was approached by a man in his 20s. He pleaded with me to give him £20 so that he could get into a night shelter. Initially I turned him down, giving him the excuse that I didn't actually have that on me in cash. He began to cry, showing me his sockless feet which he didn't have to tell me must have been like blocks of ice, though he did, repeatedly. His desperation and desolation were of an order that seemed extreme, even among the homeless people I've encountered. Eventually, I gave in and we walked to a cash machine where I withdrew the money and handed it over, but only after I had made him promise me faithfully that he would use it for the stated intention and not simply spend it on alcohol or drugs. I confess I felt bad asking him to do this. If I could have looked on at the scene, I would have wondered who this patronising character was who was making this wretched man jump through hoops before receiving his reward. But that was before I compounded matters.

As a way of testing the young man's story I had asked him which hostel he was hoping to be admitted to and he gave me the name of one near London Bridge. Once I'd passed him the machine-fresh note, I got him to assure me again that he would go straight there and check himself in. He thanked me and made off. I should have turned around there and then and headed home. Instead, I decided to carry out my own micro-survey of what happens when you give the homeless money. The sample size was, admittedly, very small but I was eager to find out whether my concerns were borne out by reality. After waiting for a minute, I began to follow him. Initially, the signs seemed encouraging: he turned down a narrow side street that I would probably have chosen myself had I needed to walk to London Bridge. I reached the corner, and continued on his trail from what I considered a safe distance. I saw him approach a woman and heard him ask if she had a cigarette she could give him. She stopped to get one out of her bag. During this procedure, he happened to look behind him but I swiftly popped myself behind a wall and out of sight. I lingered there a while to give him time to light up and move on. Just as I was about to continue my covert operation, he came round the end of the wall. Understandably peeved at being followed, he remonstrated with me in no uncertain terms before heading off down the street again. I turned the other way and started for home.

I looked up the shelter afterwards to find whether it actually existed. It did. The fact that it charged less than £10 per night didn't make me feel any less like a louse.

.·✦·.

I reached Bar Italia at ten past four. A long, brightly lit café, it had a line of high stools neatly arranged along a narrow bar on one side and a counter topped with a Gaggia coffee machine on the other. Photographs of the faces of what looked like predominantly Italian men of a certain age gazed longingly across at the glasses and bottles ranged along the wall opposite. At last I could warm my chilled hands around an espresso while soaking up the atmosphere provided by the café's free-spirited habitués. At last I could experience some of the camaraderie of the London night about which Dickens had written with such enthusiasm.

There was only one snag: Bar Italia was closed.

The website had clearly stated that the establishment was shut only between five and seven in the morning. However, the lack of either customers or proprietors, the tables stacked on top of each other and, not least, the locked door, said otherwise. My heart sank. I had been really looking forward to tasting the joys of this little piece of London history. I had also been buoyed by the anticipation of getting out of the cold for a little while. Still, there was nothing to be done. At least I now knew how

Dickens had felt when he turned up at Billingsgate to find it deserted.

In a bid to make the best of things, I retraced my steps to the café I had passed near Leicester Square with its buzz of coffee drinkers and its experimental fusion cuisine. On the way, a young Eastern European man appeared alongside me piloting one of the many bicycle rickshaws that crawl around the touristy parts of central London.

'After-party?' he asked.

'Sorry?' His accent was strong and I hadn't quite caught his words.

'After-party?' he repeated.

'Ah, well, no…but thanks for asking,' I replied.

I was quite flattered to think that I might be considered the kind of cool cat who could be found prowling the streets of Soho at gone four in the morning on the lookout for an after-party. However, on second thoughts, there were so few people out and about that he was probably asking out of sheer desperation.

I arrived at the fish-chips-falafel café only to be told that they were closing in ten minutes so I could order food or drink to take away but I couldn't sit down. After the blow I had received at Bar Italia, this follow-up jab seemed a trifle cruel. Since, in all honesty, I felt neither hunger nor thirst but merely yearned to take the weight off my feet and do some people watching, I politely declined the offer and marched on.

At Night

At Trafalgar Square, a girl scream-laughed as a boy chased her around some street furniture. The fountains beneath Nelson's Column appeared to be filled with oil. On inspection, I discovered that the deception had been caused by light reflecting off a crust of ice. It was no more than a quarter of an inch thick but had covered the entire surface of the water. I tested it with my finger and it took a couple of sturdy prods before a little hole appeared.

From a plane tree on Whitehall I heard the first birdsong of the new morning, though sunrise was still well over three hours away. It brought to mind a line in Marcel Carné's film *Les Enfants du Paradis* in which a character quips: 'The sun will be up soon. It's an early riser.' Try telling that to the birds. In winter at least they must imagine the sun to be quite a slug-a-bed.

It was immediately clear that I had penetrated a decidedly different part of London. I'd started the night in the messy, unprepossessing streets of my own patch of town. From Aldgate the roads had been overshadowed by the brash steel and glass of millions of square feet of offices and retail premises. There had been no inkling of human feeling there. That section had at last grudgingly made way for Tourist London whose defiantly happy-go-lucky bounds I had now relinquished for the austere precincts of power. I was hemmed in by grim-faced buildings housing this ministry or that, behind whose doors such deals are done and such deeds executed that, if we but knew of them, we would turn ashen-haired overnight. A policeman clutching a semi-automatic weapon stood guarding the gates of Downing Street, while in a subway underneath Parliament Square the snoring of two rough sleepers competed with Big Ben's chiming of the hour up above.

Westminster Abbey, sulking in the shadows, seemed to me a sullen and cheerless lump. I had forgotten what Dickens himself had made of it and was gratified to discover that, although he had enjoyed a little morbid fun imagining 'a wonderful procession of its dead among the dark arches and pillars', he still found the abbey itself gloomy. He had spent a quarter of an hour in quiet contemplation of the resurrection of the great and the good, which was ten minutes more than I was prepared to give it.

As with the abbey, I felt that Dickens' view of the Palace of Westminster from Westminster Bridge was one that had probably not altered greatly in the intervening years. His view of what the palace housed may be a little too Panglossian to be shared by all that many of his readers today, however. 'Regaling my houseless eyes with the external walls of the British Parliament – the perfection of a stupendous institution, I know, and the admiration of all surrounding nations and succeeding ages, I do not doubt,' though even he concedes that it was 'perhaps a little the better now and then for being pricked up to its work'.

At Night

A herring gull flew very slowly over my head as I stood on the bridge marvelling at the light show along the river to the east. This was dominated by the blood-red stylings of the London Eye and the former County Hall's cool blue. It may be pushing it to say that Earth has not anything to show more fair, as Wordsworth asserted in his sonnet, but it was nonetheless a calming array of steady coloured lights, some of which saw fit to double their appeal by reflecting themselves in the water.

When I looked up, I could see no stars at all – due in part to this same calming array I was enjoying now. Finding oneself cut off from the wonders of the night sky by the capital's appalling light pollution is one of the less attractive aspects of living there. Londoners are rarely fated to spot a shooting star arcing across the sky or sight a comet: that great harbinger of doom or augury of good, two states that I suspect depend largely on the mood of the observer. Mark Twain was born just after Halley's Comet passed by, confidently prophesied that he would leave the world when it returned, and died of a heart attack the day after the comet's nearest approach to the planet (for a change, reports of his death were not exaggerated). No Londoner is ever likely to read anything into the approach of Halley's or any other comet unless it blazes so brightly that it can be seen by day. I suspect they would be far more likely to attach significance to the unexpected reappearance in the skies of Concorde.

On seeing nothing above, I looked below. The Thames was milk-chocolate brown. Like most people, I suspect, I cannot look over the side of a bridge into a river without imagining what might happen if I tumbled into it. Eddies swirled menacingly about the piers below, hinting at the powerful undercurrents that stalk this stretch of the river patiently waiting to drag the unwary to their doom. The eldest of Dickens' ten children, also called Charles, wrote a volume called *Dickens's Dictionary of the Thames*, in which he revealed that from four to six police rowing boats went out each night to patrol the river and that 'an important portion of the duties of the Thames division consists in searching for and dealing with the bodies of suicides, murdered persons, and persons accidentally drowned'. They dragged for these unhappy individuals for just one tide, after which it was assumed that the river would have swept the cadaver away. However, 'it occasionally happens that a corpse will drift into a hole and be covered over before it becomes sufficiently buoyant to rise. Should it be eventually recovered, it is first photographed and then preserved as long as possible for identification...' It felt healthier to turn my gaze back to the lights.

South of the river for the first time, I passed around the back of the old County Hall – shut down by Margaret Thatcher and now a posh chain hotel – and caught sight of the General Lying-In Hospital across which, in big bold letters, the patronage of

At Night

'Her Majesty and Her Royal Highness the Princess of Wales' was proudly proclaimed. This imposing four-storey building was opened in 1767 and was one of a string of specialist maternity hospitals established across the country to combat high mortality rates among mothers and babies. An estimated 150,000 people began their lives here and the hospital closed as a maternity unit only as recently as 1971, so Dickens would certainly have known it. He, however, preferred to write about an altogether different hospital that stood to the southeast of here in what is now Geraldine Mary Harmsworth Park.

Bethlehem Hospital, as he calls it – it's also known as Bethlem or Bedlam, the latter being the derivation of the word we use today – was an institution set up to treat, or far more often merely confine, the mentally ill. The enormous neoclassical building sported a tremendous dome and by the time of Dickens' nocturnal visits had expanded to accommodate over 350 unfortunate souls. The novelist sought it out 'because I had a night fancy in my head which could be best pursued within sight of its walls and dome. And the fancy was this: Are not the sane and the insane equal at night as the sane lie a dreaming? Are not all of us outside this hospital, who dream, more or less in the condition of those inside it, every night of our lives?'

Had Dickens been given access to the advances in our understanding of the human mind that have been made over the last century and a half, it is doubtful he would have entertained such a notion, no matter that it clearly contained within it an attempt to empathise with those whom Victorian society was glad to see locked away. However, I think he would have enjoyed the black humour inherent in the fact that, although some of the hospital has been demolished, the section that remains was given over to house the Imperial War Museum, that testament to the madness of great tranches of mankind who would reckon themselves sane.

Waterloo station has four huge rolls of honour on its walls containing the names of the 527 London and South Western Railway Company workers who gave their lives in World War I. I scanned them for surnames from my family tree but found none – not even a Thomas, my mother's maiden name, which can usually be relied upon to offer up one or two victims.

When out walking on days when there was no market to haunt, Dickens got his fix of human contact by heading for one of London's rail termini. He would stand and watch the overnight mail trains come in, becoming absorbed in the ten minutes of frantic action that surrounded the event only to feel somewhat cheated that it was all over so quickly, leaving him alone again.

Sadly, I was a decade too late to catch the last mail train so I had to make do with whatever other excitements Waterloo had to offer at five in the morning. As it happened, I could not have chosen a more opportune time to arrive because the very first train of the day to pull out of the station is the 05.00 to Portsmouth Harbour. I would just have missed seeing it slide out but for the fact that it was a couple of minutes late in departing, a circumstance that did not, I felt, bode well for the rest of the day's timetable. There were only about half a dozen people on the large station concourse which I felt didn't bode well for passenger numbers either, given that there was a handful of other trains due to leave in the following few minutes.

Shorn of the glamour that hosting the Eurostar service briefly bestowed upon it, Waterloo has resumed its humdrum existence as a portal for commuters from the southern home counties, with only the exoticism of an Exeter or a Weymouth train to lift its spirits and allow it to dream of faraway lands where the air is clean and the sea is blue (on occasion).

I looked up at the departure boards and, imagining for a moment that I had arrived here with the aim of fleeing London with all haste, I chose my destination. Martins Heron sounded well. I would overlook the lack of an apostrophe. If I bought a ticket quick sharp and then ran hell for leather I might just about make the 05.05 stopping train to Reading, especially if that too was less than anxious to leave. I could be in Martins Heron in a little over an hour, just in time to walk out across the fields to watch the eponymous herons take off over the marshes in search of breakfast. It was only on investigation later that my fairy tale of Martins Heron came crashing around my ears. It is apparently a suburb of Bracknell, a new town that, when I last checked, still pluckily eschewed the harbouring of any pretensions to character. That 'Heron', meanwhile, is a corruption of the Old English word *hern*, meaning wasp.

The walk to Borough was peppered with small incidents. I bought a couple of doughnuts from a convenience store and gobbled them down within a minute or two of their purchase. I hadn't realised up until then that three hours or more of walking had left me somewhat peckish. An enormous poster near Southwark tube station posed the question: 'If history could be folded, where would you put the crease?' In the fug of half-formed thoughts that existed where my brain was usually kept, I couldn't tell whether this was meant to be answered or meant to be art. On reflection, I suspect it was the latter. Anyway, 1843 is the answer, as I suspect everyone knows.

Anyone in the vicinity of the Charles Dickens pub at around 5.40am would have witnessed me standing outside it to give it a little cheer. I then had to reassess my enthusiasm for a pub named after the man in whose shoes I was walking. He had seen the way the demon drink could drag men and women into the gutter – indeed, he makes an over-fondness for wine the undoing of Mr Wickfield in *David*

Copperfield – and might not be thrilled at having his name appropriated for such a venture. On the other hand, he enjoyed fame, so he might be delighted. He would certainly have been astonished at the cost of a flat in a rather ordinary-looking tower block just up the road from his pub. A sign proclaimed that a mere £765,000 would secure one of the least sought-after apartments but that you'd have to drop a far from trifling £2.75m if you wanted to get your hands on the most prestigious little box. This in a part of London that was pretty grotty back in Dickens' time and still patiently awaits its turn to become fashionable today.

I finally emerged from a passageway named Little Dorrit Court – which I'm sure would have tickled the great man – out onto Borough High Street and the two Georges. Away to my left was the George Inn while to my right rose the church of St George the Martyr, locked together in a constant battle for hearts, minds and custom.

Here I had the first sense of London awaking. Though it was still dark, a dazed-looking man was putting tables and chairs outside Nelson's Café Bar; while from somewhere above me, a blackbird chirped out its insistent song of warning, all on the one note.

I crossed the road and turned down an alleyway I had discovered only the previous spring. What seems like an ordinary enough pedestrian cut-through is actually bordered on one side by the last remaining wall of the old Marshalsea Prison. It's a place that held grim associations for Dickens for this is where his father was incarcerated as a debtor. Young Charley's mother and siblings moved into the prison as well when they could no longer afford to keep their home.

Shortly before his father's arrest, Dickens – who was then only 11 or 12 – had been taken from school and sent by his parents to support the family by earning a few shillings a week working in a boot-blacking factory. It was an experience that appears to have scarred him for life and was perhaps the well from which he drew the righteous indignation that inspired his efforts to advance the cause of the poor. He was also able to mine his memory of those times to supply characters for novels such as *Oliver Twist* and, particularly, *David Copperfield*. In the latter, the young hero finds himself abandoned when his landlord, Wilkins Micawber, winds up in the King's Bench Prison on being unable to pay his debts. It's a tribute to the author's genius that, nearly 150 years after his death, describing something as Dickensian immediately brings to mind the conditions he did so much to decry.

Dickens chose not to mention Marshalsea in the narration of his night walks, even in passing, though it was clearly on his route. Perhaps he felt he had dealt with its demons four years earlier in *Little Dorrit*, the novel in which it could be argued that Marshalsea Prison is the central character. He has left a permanent mark on the place nonetheless. Set into the paving nearby is a concrete plaque bearing the quotation: 'Melancholy streets in a penitential garb of soot, steeped the souls of the people who were condemned to look at them out of windows, in dire despondency.' The plaque leaves the lines uncredited, perhaps in the optimistic expectation that those who walk over it will recognise them as coming from Dickens' pen, even if they cannot immediately trace them to the pages of *Little Dorrit*.

We find the author instead running his hands along the rough stone of Newgate's high wall, before crossing the river to King's Bench Prison on the Borough Road, a few hundred yards to the west of Marshalsea. Here he meditates at length on the 'very curious disease [of] the Dry Rot in men' – a tendency towards idleness that he avows can bring otherwise upstanding individuals to disaster. All three prisons have long since been demolished, though Marshalsea lives on in the name of a road close by.

And so across London Bridge, underneath which the Thames had turned from milk-chocolate brown to shades of pigeon grey. The Waterside Brewery on the Surrey shore whose smells and noises so fascinated Dickens is no more, replaced now by more corporate concerns. I found myself swimming against a trickle of workers crossing to the south, bound for Borough or the stations at London Bridge. In the murky pre-dawn half-light, Tower Bridge, off to my right, did not seem its usual imperious self. The night was at its coldest – the ice on the fountains at Trafalgar Square would be thickening and perhaps even the hole I had poked would have vanished – so I quickened my pace a little as I made a beeline north for Liverpool Street.

I took a cursory wander about the station there but it was neither fish nor fowl – it was not in the berserk anthill mode that besets it every rush hour but it was also way too late to enjoy the pleasure of seeing off the first trains of the morning à la Waterloo. I turned around and crossed the road to my final landmark.

Bar Italia might have let me down, but I was certain that Polo Bar would be open, if only because it never actually closes. A greasy spoon that has recently been given a makeover, Polo, like Bar Italia, is a long and thin affair. Downstairs it sports black-and-white chequered flooring and white tiles up the walls, while upstairs high-backed padded seats form cosy booths over which plays a surprisingly hip selection of songs. None of this was of particular interest to me, however – my back had begun to hurt and I was simply looking forward to sitting down in the warm. The night had made me old.

I ordered breakfast and a pot of tea and went upstairs. I'd been here once before. On arriving at Liverpool Street sometime after midnight, I was so excited at finding a café open so late that I came in and ate an astonishingly moderate vegetable curry in the company of various other lone men. It was known

At Night

as Ponti's back then, in the dark early days of the new millennium. The café was even more of a greasy spoon but had an Italian twist, which is probably why I should have avoided the curry.

I jettisoned my hat, gloves and many layers of clothes and parked myself in a booth next to the window. My order was delivered with unsettling speed and I was soon sated and sipping tea while staring idly out of the window as the light from above gradually nudged the street lighting towards obsolescence. There was no sun, nor any a hint of it, so what natural light there was appeared as a gunmetal sludge that turned everything it touched the colour of disappointment.

At least I had some company at long last. On the table across from me four Kuwaiti boys in their late teens were comparing, in perfect, barely accented English, the dangers of London streets with those of life in Kuwait City. The latter, they concluded swiftly, was far more risky on account of all the stabbings that took place in certain parts of town. I got the impression, however, that they were all from pretty well-to-do families – my main evidence for this assertion coming from snippets of sentences such as 'he ran straight into my tennis court fence' – who didn't necessarily have to visit those parts of town if they chose not to. One of the number then embarked on a barely believable story about a serial killer whom it was believed had committed up to 500 murders. This tale was corroborated by another of the group who declared that the psychopath in question had been arrested in 2008 and executed five years later. I've been unable to dig up anything about this case, which is strange because one would have thought that such a gruesomely prolific killer would have merited at least one news item in English. However, if there is any truth to the story, it would certainly put Liverpool Street's own local operator, Jack the Ripper, in the shade.

The lads had evidently taken refuge in the café some time ago and at length considered it light enough to venture back into the safer-than-Kuwait-City streets, though none of them felt inclined to air this as the reason for their decision. One came back a few minutes later to retrieve some gloves he'd left behind and unexpectedly introduced himself to me. His name was Mike, he was 17, and he was in London, so he explained, to 'expand my craft as an actor'. He wasn't so keen on the cold though.

'I'll be doing *Twelfth Night* in Edinburgh this summer,' he told me, just in case I should find myself up there during the festival. He then shook my hand with a sort of deferential politeness that was rather charming, and made his exit, stage left.

If only Dickens had been with me, I thought – he would have relished giving the lad a few thespian pointers, leaving me to sit mutely alongside, sipping my tea and wondering whether 17 was old enough to start using phrases like 'expand my craft as an actor'.

At Night

At 7.30, a little over the Dickens-prescribed five hours, I re-cocooned myself in preparation for my walk back to Bethnal Green. This would be the point at which Dickens, having worn himself out with his wanderings, would find his body succumbing at last to the siren call of sleep. My own body, I knew, would feel no such inclination. It would rather drag me round with it for the rest of the day even though neither of us were quite all there.

I shuffled out into Bishopsgate, now busy with commuters, and pondered on things nocturnal while my feet walked me home on autopilot through familiar streets. Every night is a tiny rite of passage, I mused. We measure out our lives in single days, from the moment we wake in the morning to the moment we sleep at night. If a day goes badly, we can always hope that the night will rub the slate clean and provide a fresh start with the dawn. It's a little bit of magic that the night has been pulling off ever since humans have been around. Our part of the compact is to close our eyes and sleep so that we cannot see how the trick is done and so lose faith in it.

By the time I had thought all this, and jotted some of it down in a notebook with fingers stiff again from the cold, the day had come with all its various troubles, cares and demands. But it did not know that I had escaped.

· ★ · ·

Ten Night Rambling Tips

Over many years of wandering across country at night, I've picked up a few insights into how to do it better. I share these with you now. The fact that there's a nice round number of tips is purely accidental, though admittedly pleasing.

1. Plan your route carefully. Good places for catching big skies include the coast (though take extra care with cliff-top paths) and open areas such as moorland or fens. High vantage points with views of city lightscapes are also a bonus. Where possible, try to avoid thickly wooded areas, major roads and muddy paths.

2. Take a large-scale map, compass, head torch, some snacks and something to drink (if it gets chilly or wet, a flask of hot soup can be particularly welcome).

3. Choose a night with a big moon and, if possible, a clear sky.

4. Don't spread your possessions around you when you stop for a break. It's all too easy to mislay some small but useful piece of equipment, like a compass.

5. Use your ears and nose. You may not be able to see the stream or railway line marked on your map but you may well be able to make out the rushing of water over stones or the trundling of a late-night train. Likewise, you may be able to smell a pig farm or sense the salty ozone of the sea when both are hidden from view.

6. Wear light-coloured (or, if it's not too daunting a prospect, fluorescent) clothing in order to be seen by nocturnal drivers.

7. Try not to use your head torch too much – rather let your eyes adjust to the dark and so develop some night vision.

8. On rough ground, pick your feet up more than you would normally – it will keep you from stumbling.

9. You'll naturally walk more slowly in the dark so allow yourself more time (50 per cent more, as a rule of thumb) than you would for a day walk of similar length.

10. Go with a companion and there will be someone there to help out if you turn an ankle. If you do go by yourself, let somebody know your route beforehand.

Train Travel
Info

Here are some handy details for the train companies I used while visiting the nation's nocturnal points of interest. I took a bicycle with me and cycled from the closest station – it's the transport choice of the future.

Arriva Trains Wales
ATW covers the whole of Wales and includes the Cambrian Coast Line, which is one of the world's most scenic railway lines. The request stop Morfa Mawddach is closest to Cadair Idris, while Milford Haven is the nearest stop to Skomer.
Web: arrivatrainswales.co.uk
Tel: 0333 321 1202

East Coast
East Coast services run from London to the East Midlands, Yorkshire, Northeast England and north to Aberdeen and Inverness in the Highlands of Scotland, and will take you to Retford from where you can catch a train to Worksop and then another to Shirebrook, which is just to the west of Sherwood Forest.
Web: virgintrainseastcoast.com
Tel: 0345 722 5225

At Night

First Great Western
The FGW network includes Southwest England, South
Wales, the Cotswolds, and large parts of Southern England
including London. Head to Gunnislake for Dartmoor (be
prepared for hills).
Web: firstgreatwestern.co.uk
Tel: 0345 700 0125

Northern Rail
Northern's network spreads over the whole of Northern
England from Crewe, Stoke, Buxton and Nottingham in
the south to Carlisle and Newcastle in the north.
Web: northernrail.org
Tel: 0344 241 3454 or 0333 222 0125

ScotRail
The Caledonian Sleeper service is one of the great rail
journeys in Britain, especially if you travel all the way down
from Fort William, as I did for this book. Their trains cover
the whole of the Scottish network and some towns in
Northern England as well. Dumfries is the closest station
to the Galloway Forest Dark Sky Park. At the time of writing,
this franchise too was due to change.
Web: scotrail.co.uk
Tel: 0344 811 0141

Virgin Trains
The West Coast line from London takes in North Wales
and Scotland.
Web: virgintrains.co.uk

FURTHER USEFUL CONTACTS

National Rail Enquiries
Web: nationalrail.co.uk.

A to B Magazine
The Bike/Rail Page is full of excellent information on when and where you can travel on trains, coaches, trams and ferries with a bicycle.
Web: atob.org.uk/bike-rail

* ⋆ ★ ⋆ ⋆

Bibliography
& Websites

After Dark on Dartmoor, John Pegg; John Pegg Publishing, 1984
Charles Dickens: A Life, Claire Tomalin; Viking, 2011
Crossing's Guide to Dartmoor, William Crossing;
    David & Charles, 1965
Devonshire, D St Leger-Gordon; Robert Hale Ltd, 1950
Ghosts! Creepy Tales from Chislehurst Caves, Brian Williamson;
    Null Publishing, 2012
Night Walks, Charles Dickens; Penguin, 2010
'The Greatest Giants of Sherwood', Roger A Redfern;
    Country Life (article), 17 January 1974
*The History of the Two Impostors Lambert Simnel and Perkin
    Warbeck*, J Watts; self-published tract, 1745
The Story of an Ancient Parish: Breage with Germoe, H R
    Coulthard; Camborne Printing & Stationery Co., 1913
The Witchcraft and Folklore of Dartmoor,
    Ruth St Leger-Gordon; Alan Sutton, 1982

David Perdue's Charles Dickens Page *charlesdickenspage.com*
Endangered Species Handbook *endangeredspecieshandbook.org*
Nottinghamshire Biodiversity Action Group *nottsbag.org.uk*
Legendary Dartmoor *legendarydartmoor.co.uk*
Newman Family Tree *newman-family-tree.net*
EarthSky *earthsky.org*
London School of Cycling *londonschoolofcycling.co.uk*
Warsop Web *warsopweb.co.uk*

Author's Acknowledgements

All the staff at the British Library's Rare Books
Reading Room.
David and Rosemary Robertson of Moniaive.
Everyone at Gloucestershire Against Badger Shooting –
especially Olivia, Ella, Lizzie, Josie, Wilf and Mr Badger –
all power to your collective elbows.
James Davis at First Great Western.
Jannine Russell at ScotRail.
John Gelson at East Coast.
Joselyn Rankin at Northern Rail.
Kim and Nick Hoare for looking after me post-
Dunwich Dynamo.
Lee Wright of Meden Vale for rescuing me in
Sherwood Forest.
Lewis Brencher at Arriva Trains Wales.
Melissa Harrison for her customary nature brilliance.
Everyone at Skomer, especially Ollie Padget for his
excellent Manx shearwater skills, help with the manuscript
and a fantastic night.
Steve and Sheila Chattaway on Piel Island for their
company, delicious vegan food and great stories.
The Gentle Mole for information on Welbeck Park.
Tracy Clifton at Virgin Trains.
My particular appreciation goes to Lisa-Raine, Jackson and
Oscar Hunt, in whose flat much of this book was written;

At Night

and to Damian and Renu Basher, in whose *buco* this book was amended and polished.

I would also like to thank my agent Ben Mason.

Finally, I would like to thank Tom Bromley for his editorial advice and encouragement. Special thanks go to Helen Brocklehurst who, like a master sculptor, looked at the block of stone that was the manuscript and lopped off everything that didn't look like this book; and to Donna Wood, who blew my nose and then expertly helped me chisel in the detail.